LIFE

IN HALF A SECOND

How to achieve **success**
before it's too late

Matthew Michalewicz

Published by Hybrid Publishers

Melbourne Victoria Australia

© Matthew Michalewicz 2013

www.hybridpublishers.com.au

First published 2013

National Library of Australia Cataloguing-in-Publication entry

Michalewicz, Matthew, author.

Life in half a second : how to achieve success before it's too late / Matthew Michalewicz.

ISBN: 978-0-9922861-0-1 (paperback)

Includes bibliographical references.

Subjects: Success; Conduct of life; Life skills.

Dewey Number: 158

Cover design by Rachael Harding / Ennovative

To my incredible, unbelievable family:

Babi, Didi, Lula, Krecik, Guinea-Rabbit, Boo-Boo, and Pixie.

And with heartfelt thanks to:

*Constantin Chiriac, Larisa Stamova, Darryl Schafferius,
James Balzary, Polly McGee, Stuart Snyder,
Kishen Vijayadass, Mike Richards, Susan Andrews,
Doug Misener, Nanette Moulton, Winston Broadbent,
and Colin Pearce.*

Contents

My six-year-old son asks, "Dad, why do you have to write this book?"

"I don't *have* to," I explain. "I *want* to."

"But *why?*"

"Because it gives me pleasure to write it."

"But *how?*"

"Because this book is everything that I am. And in a hundred years, I'll be long gone, but this book will still be here and your children's grandchildren can read it and be with me."

"I don't understand."

I pause; rethink my strategy. "Okay, let me explain it another way. How do you feel when you're skateboarding?"

"Happy," he replies, the corners of his mouth turning upwards.

"Well, that's how I feel when I'm writing this book."

Silence, contemplation. His eyes widen and he stares deeply into my soul. "Dad, are you writing a book about *skateboards?*"

"Life is short and death is long."
Fritz Shoulder

The Countdown

Everyone knows that life is short – it's the most over-preached truth on earth. But how short is it, *exactly*?

Planet Earth is four-and-a-half *billion* years old. The species you and I belong to, Homo sapiens, did not emerge until some 200,000 years ago. The oldest known fossils of modern humans are only 160,000 years old, discovered in Herto, Ethiopia. So out of the four-and-a-half *billion* years that this planet has been floating through the nothingness of space, we've been around some .0044% of that time. Put another way, if our planet was exactly one year old, then modern humans would have only been around for the last 23 *minutes*. Measured on the same scale, if our planet was a year old, then your entire life would amount to *half a second*.

In planet-time, that's all you have: half a second.

We don't appreciate this as kids. Time seems unlimited

and goes by ever so slowly. We're impatient to grow up, become adults, and enter the real world. We imagine all the freedom we'll have, all the things we'll get to do. But when adulthood finally arrives, we discover that we'll be spending the vast majority of our "freedom" at work, paying bills, surviving, often in jobs we don't like or don't care about. Life is not how we imagined it and disillusionment sets in. We spend our half second doing everything except what we really want, dreaming of the future, of some distant, faraway day when life will be different, better, when we can finally do the things we want. But as we grow older, time begins moving faster and faster, and our long-awaited day never seems to come.

The tragedy of life isn't that we only have half a second. *The tragedy is that we waste it.* In my travels across continents, countries, and cultures, first as a serial immigrant and later as a businessman, I met people from every walk of life imaginable. And throughout all these journeys in different parts of the globe, I became obsessed by a single question:

What would you do if you only had one year to live?

I'm not sure where the question came from, what prompted it or why, but it quickly became my favorite topic of conversation. And the more I asked the question – to people of varying backgrounds, skin color, religion, and education – the more obsessed I became. *Why?* Because I always received the same answer. With

2

only a year to live, most people would quit work, spend time with family, see the world, and do everything they always dreamed of doing *before it's too late.* Their answers would be thick with emotion – not sadness or regret, but enthusiasm, eagerness. I felt they were about to set sail on some journey they often fantasized about but never actually took. With heat and fervor, eyes flashing, gleeing almost, they spoke of the many things they would do before death claimed them. And after the hundredth question and hundredth answer, I finally thought, *Good God! Can we only live when we're dying?*

My impression of the world is that we spend life doing what we "have to" rather than what we "want to." This comes across in many psychology and happiness studies, especially those related to work. Harvard studies show that worker happiness is at an all-time low,[1] with 74% of employees wanting to find a new line of work.[2] At heart, *we would rather be doing something else.* A number of prominent psychologists have proclaimed that every industrialized nation is experiencing an epidemic of depression,[3] all the way from university students – where a study of 13,500 students found that 94% felt overwhelmed by

---

1   Riggio, R., "Why Happiness at Work is Declining," *Psychology Today*, 25 October 2010

2   Hall, A., "I'm Outta Here! Why 2 Million Americans Quit Every Month," *Forbes*, 3 March 2013

3   Lambert, C., "The Science of Happiness," *Harvard Magazine*, February 2007

everything they had to do and 45% were too depressed to function properly[4] – to the general population, where only 28% of people out of a massive sample of 520,000 were classified as "emotionally well off" as defined by positive and negative daily emotions, as well as a clinical diagnosis of depression.[5] What can we make of all these studies and statistics?

One thing: *we would rather be doing something else.*

And that, right there, is the great tragedy of human existence. While this planet has been spinning and forming and cooling for *billions* of years, nature has been busy making *you*. From scraps of living matter – from bacteria, microbes, fermenting cells fighting for the right to exist, squirming and striving, growing in complexity through millions of generations, learning to breathe, mutating, spawning life on land and sea and air against the backdrop of centuries and millennia passing – the first genus Homo emerged. Somehow – only God knows how – he rose from the mess of biology and creation, covered in slime, ignorant and animalistic, and learned to stand, walk, stare at the sky, marvelling at the dark voids and cosmic dust above. And then he embarked upon the journey of all journeys, the hundred-thousand-generation epic of

---

4   Kadison, R., "Getting an Edge – Use of Stimulants and Antidepressants in College," *New England Journal of Medicine*, September 2005
5   Rheault, M., McGeeney, K., "Emotional Health Higher Among Older Americans," *Gallup Wellbeing*, 12 August 2011

survival, of hunting and being hunted, overcoming frost, famine, struggling with tools made of wood and stone, discovering fire, migrating tens of thousands of miles to colonize the world, living by the law of fist and club, coping with violence, rape, conquest, disease without cures, starvation – enduring unthinkable pain and suffering so that the species could survive – living with the sole intent to mate, procreate, pass genes on to the next generation of survivors, over and over, thousands and thousands and thousands of times, until finally, at the very end of that endless ladder, one sperm out of 300 million attached itself to an egg, creating *you*, only *you*.

The point of it all, since the planet cooled and nature first put her hand to work, was to produce *you* – the finest specimen of an eternity of mutation and adaptation, surviving the evolutionary climb of all evolutionary climbs, through miracle and chance, beating all odds, winning a trillion-to-one-wager, winning the sperm race to be born, to be *you*. And today, sitting comfortably, reading this book, safe, warm, fed, the beneficiary of millions of years of unimaginable suffering and billions of years of incalculable good luck, there *you* are, with just half a second to enjoy the result, the marvel of existing, the miracle of *being*. And what do you do with that half second? *Something other than what you want!*

It's the tragedy of all tragedies – it makes Shakespearean blank verse seem comic by comparison. Our lives are so cluttered doing what we "have to" that there's no room for what we "want to," even though we only have half a second to do it. Perhaps that's why there's so much unhappiness in the world! Perhaps that's why Americans spend $57 *billion* on lottery tickets each year[6] – not to win wealth, but to win freedom and finally do the things they *want to*.

But what are we waiting for?

If we only had one year to live, our desire to start living – to use what's left of our half second to the fullest – would become unstoppable and we would finally, finally, take action. *But is that what it takes?* Must we be confronted with death to finally do the things we want? *Is that what we're waiting for?* Sadly, it seems so. Death always seems a long way off, a concept almost, as remote and abstract as the dark side of the moon. We don't appreciate our mortality or fully comprehend how little time we have, so we defer our desires for another day. It's not until death becomes more tangible, inevitable, that we realize our time is measured and we spring into action.

We're relaxed and laid back about the time we have left because we measure our age in "years lived." We know that 50 is older than 40, and 40 is older than 30, but so what? What does that really tell us? Not much. It's like knowing how many gallons a car has used without

---

6   Krasny, J., Lubin, G., Sprung, S., "12 Ways Americans Throw Away Money," *Business Insider*, 1 October 2012

knowing how many gallons are left. The most important information is missing. So what would happen if we measured our age in "days left" rather than "years lived"? I bet we wouldn't be as relaxed and laid back. I bet that death would become less abstract. Let's try it.

The average life expectancy of the global population in 2011 is 70 years,[7] ranging from 80+ years in countries such as Japan, Australia, and France, to less than 60 years in South Africa, Laos, and Kenya.[8] Let's assume you live in one of the sixteen countries where life expectancy is more than 80 years, or that you'll beat the odds and live to be 80. In either case, subtract your current age from 80 and multiply the result by 365. This is the number of "days left" you have – assuming all goes well and you don't find yourself on the wrong end of "average." I'm currently 37 years old, so $80 - 37 = 43$, and $43 \times 365 = 15{,}695$ days. So that's it. That's all I have left: *15,695 days.* And there's something more meaningful about "15,695 days left" than "37 years old." I feel a sense of urgency, haste. *There's a countdown on my life.*

Perhaps that's why people accuse me of being in a hurry. I don't need to be. But I am. *Why?* Because it took a billion years for me to get here, and now that I'm here, I've only got half a second to make the most of it. So yes, I admit it, I'm in a hurry! *I'm in a hurry to live.* The world is right there,

---

7   World Health Organization, 2012
8   www.WorldLifeExpectancy.com

outside my window, in the blueness of the sky, over the horizon, begging to be discovered, touched, appreciated. It's all there waiting for me – *so what am I waiting for?*

"I'm here to live, man, live!" I remind myself each morning.

I want to lie in the grass, underneath the burning sun and swirling clouds, wind blowing, seasons changing, with the raw earth under my fingernails. From the largeness of the cosmos to the smallness of my little toe, I love life. And knowing that everything is ephemeral, fleeting, here one moment and gone the next, I'm not saving anything for later. *There might not be a "later."* Like the great motivators that preach from stadiums and pulpits, I want to *live full and die empty.* I've skydived, explored the great pyramids, sat next to the Moai on Easter Island, bungee jumped, owned Ferraris, driven at 180 mph, rock climbed above Machu Picchu, sailed the Mediterranean, scuba dived on wrecks in the Caribbean, photographed the Nazca Lines from a light plane, touched the giant tortoises on the Galapagos Islands, met the Pope, worked with Lech Walesa, and dined with Arnold Schwarzenegger – I'm not waiting for anything. Each morning I tell my wife and kids how much I love them, as if I'll never see them again – each year I'm living like it's my last, bucket list and all.

Do you have a bucket list? No? Then make one and do it *now*, while you still can, while there's still life and strength in your veins. If you only had one year to live, *you'd do it now.* Nothing would stop you. No amount of commitments, obligations, or responsibilities. But because you measure time in "years lived" rather than "days left," the future seems unlimited, so you defer and wait. You do everything you "have to" and very little of what you "want to." But what are you waiting for? *When you're old and frail? When your desire has evaporated? When your loved ones are gone?*

The tragedy of life is *waiting* and *deferring*. I see people doing it every day, everywhere I go, in airports, restaurants, factories, offices, classrooms – waiting and deferring. I see it on their faces, in their eyes. They believe they've got all time in the world, so they wait and defer, putting off the things they "want to" for another time, for "later." And when later comes, they often feel it's too late – that they've waited and deferred for too long. But why continue to wait and defer because you're older today than you were yesterday? What sense does that make? You won't have any more "days left" tomorrow than you do today. What's left is what's left, and you must make the most of it.

Harlan David Sanders certainly made the most of his "days left." After a colorful life that included farming, piloting steamboats, and selling insurance, he founded Kentucky Fried Chicken at the age of 65, immortalizing his eleven herbs and spices and becoming a multi-millionaire in the process.[9] Ray Kroc did the same, beginning his legendary transformation of McDonald's into a global colossus while he was in his 50s. There are thousands of similar stories, as evidenced by entrepreneurial statistics. Consider that the "over 55" category is responsible for starting 28% of all new businesses in the United States each year.[10] The truth is that it's only "too late" when you're dead. That's the only time when it's truly too late. Any time before that, the dice are still in play, the dealer still has cards to deal, and you still have time.

It's not over till it's over.

But you don't have any time to waste, nobody does. If you want more from life than the daily grind of work, routine, retirement, and death, you've only got half a second to do it. To achieve success and turn your dreams into reality, *the only time you'll ever have is now.* And that's where this book comes in. Based on scientific research and thousands of real-world studies, *Life in Half a Second* is your master key to success. Free from gimmicks, mind tricks, fairy tales, and wishing upon stars, it will help you achieve success before it's too late, *before you're dead.*

I have organized *Life in Half a Second* into five "doors of success," which represent the absolute essence and dis-

---

9   Rosofsky, I., "Adventures in Old Age," *Psychology Today*, 10 February, 2010
10 US Small Business Administration, 2010

tilment of success – what makes it possible and what you must do to achieve it. Every motivational book you read, every gravity-defying success story you hear – whether it's climbing Mount Everest, becoming a billionaire, setting a world record, or making a scientific breakthrough – is based on these five doors. There is nothing more. If you want something in life, these five doors are the only way to get it. And whether you are my son or a stranger, I will give you the same advice: read this book, do what it says. *Success will follow.*

I don't know who you are, where you live, or anything about your values or background. But I do know one thing: *you've only got half a second.* And you might be content to use that half second waiting and deferring, waiting and deferring – never quite knowing why or what for. *But not me.* I want to close my eyes knowing I made the most of life – knowing I never waited and I never deferred. If I had more time, I would have done more. But with the time I had, I did all I could. That's why I'm in a hurry; that's why I don't have a moment to lose. *There's a countdown on my life.*

And guess what ... *there's a countdown on yours as well.*

*"It's not a disgrace to not reach the stars, but it's
a disgrace to have no stars to reach for."*
Benjamin Mayes

The First Door

A South African boy died tragically while looking for water in a cave. With so many deaths and tragedies in the world, chances are you didn't hear about it. But you should. The story is quite amazing and his remains were just recently found.

In the dead of night, with the moon hiding its face behind a shroud of heavy clouds, a brutal thirst roused the boy from sleep. He tried swallowing the hard lump in his throat, but couldn't − he had nothing to swallow with. Each breath hurt, burning and scorching its way through his lungs. Next to him, at the entrance of the cave, slept his mother. He knew there was water inside the cave, dewdrops that had rolled off the walls and collected in dark pools at the bottom. All he had to do was go inside and get them.

But it was dangerous.

His mother had warned him against going in the cave. For a moment, he weighed his mother's words against his thirst. *His thirst was overwhelming.*

"I'll be very careful," was how he justified his disobedience. *"Very careful."*

He rose from the ground and began groping his way along the cold walls. Tired, stiff from sleep, he walked on in utter darkness. The sharp rocks on the ground grew loose and began to cut his feet.

"Just a little farther," he whispered to himself.

But before he could take another step, a deep growl tore through the blackness ahead. Startled, afraid, he spun around but lost his balance in the act. The ground gave way underneath and for a moment he was weightless, lighter than air. His stomach touched his throat and a blast of wind rushed through his hair. He was falling, fast, into darkness and terror. He heard a tumble, snap, and then a loud crack. His head had found the bottom of the shaft. That much he knew. And a moment later, he knew nothing more.

Daylight came and went, then came and went many times over the years that followed. Time passed, the landscape changed, grass grew where it had never grown before, until the cave disappeared along with the boy's remains, forgotten.

On a similarly hot day in August 2008, Professor Lee Berger and his son were exploring the rolling hills north of Johannesburg. It was still morning when they stumbled upon the mouth of a hidden cave. Concealed by grass, rocks, and time itself, they crawled inside. Much eroded, the once deadly shaft was now a gentle slope easily accessible to the pair. The son was ahead of the father when he tripped on something on the ground. He reached down and grabbed a thin, yellowish-grey stick. His eyes widened with comprehension.

"Dad, I found a fossil!" he yelled.

Lost and forgotten, the boy was now found by another boy of the same age. The two boys, one dead in the ground, the other very much alive, standing over him, lived two million years apart – *two million years had passed*. Professor Lee Berger and his son also found the boy's mother, who had gone looking for him, along with the bones of a sabre-toothed cat, whose growl had sparked the chain of events almost two million years ago.[11] The first downpours of the rainy season had swept the bodies into a pool of water rich with lime and sand, which cemented them in place, like a time machine. *National Geographic* hailed the discovery as "one of the greatest fossil finds of all time."[12]

As I said earlier, the story is amazing. Not because the well-preserved bones provide a rare glimpse into

11 "New Hominid Species Discovered in South Africa," *New York Times*, 9 April 2010

12 National Geographic: http://natgeotv.com/asia/the-two-million-year-old-boy

our history, into the making of mankind, but because it makes us realize, in the most painful of ways, that life is a time-tick against the vastness of eternity – *that millions of years will pass after we die.* For the boy and his mother, so many years came and went that the very nature of our species changed a dozen times, until finally a Homo sapien boy made the discovery. With air in our lungs, time isn't in much of a hurry. Minutes and hours stretch themselves into days, weeks, and months. But once the air is gone, time moves a lot faster – like when we're asleep. The years roll forward into millennia, then eras, epochs, eons, and finally, eternity. At some point, so much time will pass that our Sun will stop burning and die.

There's no question that life is but a moment, a snap of the fingers. The real question is: *what are you going to do with that moment?*

What You Want

The shortness of life is sobering, scary. I'm afraid of the future, knowing that at some point consciousness will cease, while loved ones and their loved ones, and all the cherished things of life, move on, through time, without me.

But the shortness of life also motivates me – it motivates me to do something with it, make the most of it. And the only way I can make the most of my half second is by being absolutely clear about what I want.

This brings us to the first door of success, *Clarity*.

Successful people get what they want out of life because they *know* what they want. To achieve success, you must know what success looks like. You must define it. I can tell you as fact, as certitude, that you won't wander your way to success. Without clarity, without knowing what you want, your life will be an accident – however pleasant or unpleasant, an accident nonetheless. It wasn't planned or intended, it just happened. And without clarity, the rest of this book is meaningless. If you don't know what you want, how can this book help you? How can *any* book help you? – *help you do what exactly?*

To unlock the Door of Clarity, you must define what success means for *you* – what you want in life – and you must define it as *a goal*. This makes the definition of success easy, simple: *success = goal attainment*. You will achieve success by achieving your goals, whatever they may be. And because we are a melting pot of cultures, upbringings, values, biases, and more, it's unsurprising that we have different goals: from scientific research, sporting records, financial independence, a happy marriage, career advancement, building a business, balancing family and work, to helping the poor. But even though our goals are different, the definition of success remains the same: *success = goal attainment*.

I have read many books and heard many speakers claim that you must "think big" to achieve success, or that "people fail in life not because they aim too high and miss, but because they aim too low and hit."[13] I disagree with both these statements. Success is not defined by thinking big or small, or aiming high or low. Success is defined by what you aim for – *by what goals you set*. If you think big, aim high, and set large goals, then your success will be large. If you think small, aim low, and set small goals, then your success will be small. But in either case, it's still success. People fail in life not because they aim high or low, *but because they don't aim at all.*

"Success" and "financial success"

Although we can define success in any number of ways through the goals we set, most of us still think of success in terms of money. *Why?* Because money affects every area of our life – from the food we eat and clothes we wear, to the quality of our education and medical care. Money is a central pillar of our modern existence, as real as the next house payment. And because most people don't earn enough for all their needs and wants, they go without, deprived, always thinking of success in the context of dollars and cents.

Consider that in Australia, where I live, one in five people would struggle to come up with $1,000 to deal with an emergency, and one in three people spend every

---

13 Les Brown and the late Bob Moawad, among many others.

cent they earn.[14] *Think about that:* 20% of the population would struggle to scrape a thousand bucks together for an unexpected event, and a third of the population is living hand-to-mouth from paycheck to paycheck.

In the United States, the statistics are even worse: 30% of workers have less than $1,000 in savings and investments;[15] almost 50 million Americans are on food stamps, struggling to exist below the breadline;[16] and one in five people are uninsured, without subsidized access to basic health care.[17]

And even that pales in comparison to global statistics, where one in seven people go to bed hungry, dreaming of dinner, trying to ignore the gnawing pain in their stomach, while more than 20,000 children die *each day* due to lack of food.[18] For these people, money means bread, shelter, survival. They need to eat to live, and to eat, they need money. The reality of money is impossible to escape, and so it's unsurprising that so many people think of "success" and "financial success" as synonyms.

But irrespective of what success means to you at a personal, individual level – whether it's a million dollars

---

14 "One in Five Aussies Struggle to Find $1000," *Business Spectator*, 17 February 2013

15 Employee Benefit Research Institute, 2012

16 Food Research and Action Center (FRAC)

17 National Health Interview Survey, 2011

18 World Hunger and Poverty Facts and Statistics, 2012, www.World Hunger.org

or an Olympic gold medal – you're more likely to achieve success by having *goals*. More than 80 years of research has consistently shown that we achieve more when we set goals.[19] In fact, the effectiveness of goal-setting has been proven in studies involving more than 40,000 male and female participants in Asia, Europe, and North America, using time spans from one minute to 25 years at the individual, group, and organizational level.[20] Recent studies by Professor Dave Kohl at Virginia Tech University found that people with goals *earn nine times as much* over their lifetime as people without goals.

Power of mental focus

There isn't a motivational speaker on the planet who doesn't advocate goal-setting. And it's not just the speakers: read the biographies of the ultra-successful, and you won't get far before stumbling upon their use of goals to achieve success. Whether it's Arnold Schwarzenegger, Jack Welch, Warren Buffet, Richard Branson, Barack Obama, or Bill Gates – they all advocate the use of goals. I'd be hard pressed to point out a single person

---

19 Cecil Alec Mace conducted the first empirical studies in 1935, and is credited as "being the man who discovered goal-setting." Edwin Locke further refined goal-setting theory in the 1960s, and his article "Toward a Theory of Task Motivation and Incentive" in 1968 established the connection between goals and performance.

20 Locke, E. & Latham, G. *New Directions in Goal-Setting Theory*, Association of Psychological Science, 2006

who achieved success without setting goals. And there's a reason behind the persuasiveness of goals: *they work.* There are many reasons why, but one of the most compelling is that goals channel your efforts and behaviors in a particular direction.[21] Put another way, once you have a clear goal, you begin thinking about it, and by thinking about it, you narrow your attention and efforts to activities related to the goal. *You start moving towards the goal.*

That's why goals are so powerful – *they allow your mind to focus.* On a daily basis, your attention is spread across a million moments. Friends, family, laughing, loving, sitting in traffic, work, working out, stress, chores, hobbies, bills, dreaming – without end, every day. And when you chill in front of the television, when the revolving door pauses for a moment, your brain is overpowered by a media tsunami that scrambles your thoughts. Goals cut through the noise. Goals dim the background. Goals pull focus on what matters. Everything else grows a little less clear, a little less important.

In many psychology books, an interesting exercise is presented about the power of attention and focus. The book asks the reader to stop reading, look around the room, and memorize everything *red*. If you haven't done this exercise before, try it now. To make the task easier,

---

21 Cummings, T. & Worley, C. *Organizational Development & Change*, South Western Educational Publishing, 2004

you can list the red items on a piece of paper. When done, close your eyes, and without opening them, recall all the *green* items in the room. You will struggle – most people struggle – which is the point of the exercise. It demonstrates how your mind's attention and focus works. People can't recall things that were in plain sight just a few moments before, because their mind was focused on something else.

This phenomenon is referred to as "Reticular Activation" – a fancy name for your mind's ability to filter out irrelevant information and concentrate on essentials. Reticular Activation has kept our species alive and away from extinction by allowing us to focus on threats, food sources, and mating opportunities. In modern society, you'll notice this process when you buy a new car, and immediately see plenty of similar cars on the road when you had never seen any before. That's Reticular Activation at work, focusing your mind. This basic psychological principle is behind much of the power of goals. Instead of having your attention scattered across the day-to-day ongoings of life, you zoom in on what matters.

Precision

For goals to be effective – for your mind to be able to focus on them – they must be "precise." *But I know precisely what I want!* I can almost hear you say. *I want to be rich, I want to be happy, I want to be successful.* But what does "rich, happy, successful" really mean? No one knows for sure. Such words are concepts, fuzzy as foghorns, *the very opposite of precise.* They're difficult to grasp unless you express them in numbers – dates, percentages, units, dollars. People understand numbers; they're not elusive, they're not fuzzy – they cut through the fog. That's why mathematics is such a universal language – the only language shared by all human beings, regardless of culture, religion, or gender. And why business plans are always expressed in numbers: *We will achieve X growth by Y date; we will capture X of the market within Y years.*

Can you imagine the management team of a major corporation planning to achieve *good profits and lots of customers*? Shareholders would laugh them out of the room. And yet, most people define their future in such loose, meaningless terms.

It's like asking me to get some of "that stuff" from the supermarket.

"Come on, you know, that *stuff,*" you say.

"What *stuff*?" I reply.

I don't have a clue what you're talking about. I don't know what to look for or where to look. But if you ask me to buy "vanilla yogurt, the one with the blue and white label at the back of aisle four, top shelf," then no problem, I can do that. I know what I'm looking for and where to look.

Success cannot be "that stuff." It must be the "vanilla yogurt." Instead of wanting to "lose weight," set a goal of losing ten pounds in two months. One goal is "that stuff"; the other is "vanilla yogurt." Go further, and make the goal ten pounds *of fat*, as many dieters tend to shed more water and muscle than actual fat. Your goal now has a blue and white label and is sitting on aisle four.

Instead of wanting your business to become a "market leader," set a goal of capturing 15% of tier-1 customers and 25% of tier-2 customers in your home market over the next two years. Instead of wanting to "spend more time with your kids," set a goal of spending two hours of uninterrupted, phone-off, quality time with them each day. Be specific, be *precise*.

One of my favorite stories about precise goals comes from Jim Carrey, star of *Dumber and Dumber*, *The Mask*, *Ace Ventura*, and numerous other blockbuster movies. Everyone knows about his success, but what few people know is that in 1987, when Jim Carrey was an unknown actor struggling to make ends meet, he wrote a check to himself for $10 million for "acting services rendered" with a future date of 28 November 1995. For years he carried that check around in his wallet, keeping his goal firmly in sight, until he was paid $10 million in 1994 to star in *Dumb and Dumber*.[22] It probably took Jim Carrey

---

22 O., A., The Jim Carrey Show, *Salon*, 8 December, 1999

less than a minute to define his goal on a post-dated check. But in the years ahead, that check provided his mind with a focal point, a green light towards which he steered his life.

Precision not only makes your goals more measureable (like *$10 million* in *eight* years or *ten* pounds in *two* months), but also brings them to life in your mind – it allows you to *see* them. When you're going to sleep at night, your head sinking, eyelids heavy, it's difficult to see "happy." But if your goal is to become a movie star, living in the public eye, with homes on beaches and faraway hills and the lifestyle that goes with it – that's something you can literally close your eyes and see. Precision makes it real, providing your mind with a mental beacon to pull towards.

The key to the Door of Clarity is to *set precise goals.*

Visualization

One of the most famous goal-setters of all time is Arnold Schwarzenegger. His girlfriend from the late 60s, Barbara Outland, wrote an endearing book about their early days together.[23] In it, she described Arnold as a "prolific goal-setter," somebody who sat at his desk on January 1st and wrote goals for the year ahead on index cards. He would write things like "starting a mail order

---

23 Outland, B. *Arnold and Me: In the Shadow of the Austrian Oak*, Author-house, 2006

business, winning the Mr Olympia, buying a new car." On December 31st, he would be back at the same desk, putting the index cards away, one by one, with the word "Done" on top. Year on year, without fail, he precisely defined his goals.

Arnold was also a great proponent of visualizing goals. He would fall asleep with a filmstrip of winning contests, heaving weights, coming to America, and more, burning under his eyelids. And there's a reason why Arnold and millions of other athletes and businesspeople advocate the use of visualization: *it's scientifically proven to work.* Brain studies show that visualization impacts many cognitive processes, such as motor control, attention, perception, and memory, preparing your brain for actual performance.[24] So when you visualize an act, your brain tells your neurons to "perform" the act, creating a new neural pathway that primes your body to perform in a way consistent with what you imagined.

The easier your goals are to see, the more attainable they will seem. And research shows that people who visualize goals are more successful in achieving them.[25] When Andre Agassi won Wimbledon, he said it was like *déjà vu*

---

24 Levan, A., "Seeing is Believing: The Power of Visualization," *Psychology Today*, 3 December 2009

25 Grohol, J., "Visualize Your Goal in Order to Attain It," *PsychCentral*, 16 August 2011

because he had won it in his mind countless times.[26] For this reason, make your goals so clear and precise that you can *see* them, *feel* them, and *hear* them. Each night, every night, spend a few minutes visualizing your goals. Not "thinking" about them, but actually *seeing* them. From the delicious tightness of an engagement ring, searing sand of distant lands, laughter of children, to your boss' voice delivering praise and promotion – such goals will move you, pull you.

Design Your Life

As a modern society, we can design almost anything, from complex satellites in space, to advanced medical devices, to atomic bombs. We can also change our environment to suit our needs, through the construction of dams, bridges, rivers, lakes, canals, and more. Even at an individual level – at a "me and you" level – we can design our homes, clothes, computers, cars, right down to the speed of the processor and color of the steering wheel.

I have often wondered – and my journey to understanding success began with this question – *why can't we do the same thing with our lives?* Why can't we "design" our careers, hobbies, the amount of free time we have? Why can't we say that we want our lives to look like *so and so*

---

26 Afremow, J., "Visualize to Actualize," *Psychology Today*, 13 September, 2011

and make it happen? What's the difference? We're enormously proactive in designing and configuring the things we buy so that they're exactly the size, shape, color, we want. But when it comes to life, we are far less proactive. We become resigned to things being a certain way, thinking they will always be a certain way, and we let the tide of our day-to-day routine pull us into a future not of our choosing or making.

But it doesn't have to be that way. You *can* have the life you want. You *can* design it, build it, and step into it. Designing your life is no different to sculpting, painting, or writing: day by day, piece by piece, you turn what's in your mind into reality. And by committing your goals to paper, you're taking the first step in that process. By using precise goals to describe what you want in life, you're providing your mind with something to focus on – which is the starting point of achieving success and designing the life you want.

How to be 1 in 100

Given that goal-setting is quick, costs nothing, and is proven to get you closer to the things you want in life, you'd think everybody would be doing it. And yet, the opposite is true. Consider that out of 100 people in the United States, on average, 80 don't have any goals; 16 have goals but don't write them down; 3 have goals, write them down, but don't review them; and only one person in a hundred has goals, writes them down, and reviews them.[27] With so few people setting goals, you'd think we've reached Utopia as a society. Life must be so grand that goals have become passé. The average person must already have everything they've ever dreamed of, right? With the number of people falling below the poverty line growing *75 times* faster than job growth, this certainly is not the case.[28]

So what's going on? With 50 million Americans living in poverty, why is only 1% of the population setting goals, writing them down, and reviewing them? Why are the most needy not doing the simplest, most time-tested, proven, and cost-effective (free!) thing to help themselves?[29] Explain it to me. I don't understand. *Is it because they enjoy hunger? Because they choose to go without?* It doesn't make sense. If you sat them down and asked, *Would you like to have more financial security? A better job? More time for your kids?* each and every one of them would say *Yes!* and yet, they don't even take the first step towards making it happen.

Taking an index card and writing, *Goal 1: $2000 financial buffer by year-end*, would increase the probability of

27 Professor Dave Kohl, Virginia Tech University

28 "Food Stamp Growth 75X Greater than Job Creation," *Weekly Standard*, November 2012

29 Even if the top 1% of goals setters were all in poverty and part of the 50 million on food stamps, it still leaves 47 million people in poverty that are not setting, writing, and reviewing goals, as 1% of the US population is just over 3 million people

this happening by orders of magnitude. The simple act of writing it down, of casting desires into written words, immediately increases the odds of success. And yet, most people can't be bothered; even those in the deepest of need. *Why?* Perhaps they don't know about goal-setting? Perhaps they don't believe it will work? As I said earlier, I don't know why. But what I do know is that *you* know about goal-setting. In the *Action Items* section at the end of this chapter, I want you to define your goals, write them down, and review them regularly. By doing this, you'll automatically be in the top 1% of goal-setters – you'll be firmly through the Door of Clarity and on your way.

But if you refuse – if you can't commit a single goal to paper – if you can't do something that straightforward, that simple, then do the next best thing: stop reading this book and give it to somebody else. Don't read any more. You won't succeed. Not because you're not capable, not because you're not smart enough or good enough – you won't succeed because you *choose* not to succeed. I'm not asking you to bet your life savings on the roulette wheel. I'm not asking you to spend five years away from home in search of truth and meaning. I'm not asking you to fast for 40 days and 40 nights. All I'm asking is for a couple of sentences on a piece of paper! If that's too much to ask – to define a goal and put it on paper – then what's the point of this book? *What's the point of reading further?*

I believe in free will. I believe in choice. Every moment of every day, each of us has choice. *You have a choice right now.* You are standing in front of the first door of success – you know where it is, and what's required to get through. You also know that you've only got half a second and there's no time to waste. What happens next is up to you. You can say, *you know, this all sounds like nonsense. I don't care what 80 years of research says – I'm not doing any of it!* You can then close this book, put it away in a safe place, and life will continue just as before. Nothing will be different. You don't *want* it to be different.

Or, you can make another choice. You can say, *you know what, there's something here, something that could improve my life. I'll give it a go. What do I have to lose?* In either case, the *choice* is yours. It's your half second.

So what are you going to do?

You still here? Good.

You are *choosing* to be here; you are committing to do what I ask. You are going to define your goals, write them down, and review them. And then you're going to do something more, something that will give you an edge over the top 1% of goal-setters: you're going to *share* your goals with other people.

Why?

Because it creates commitment. When you tell somebody you'll do something, you're far more likely to do it.

Research on goal-setting demonstrates that people who share their goals with others are more likely to succeed over people who just write goals, or worse, just think them.[30] It's empowering to say, *I will do this, it's my goal, it's my dream.* It sounds powerful, formidable. The more you hear yourself say it, the more you'll commit to it.

Speak!

Telling people your goals, much like writing them down, is simple, quick, and proven – a *must do* – and yet again, few people do it. And it's not just goal-setting – most of us have difficulty in expressing our true feelings on a day-to-day basis. Perhaps we want to avoid awkwardness, embarrassment, or maybe we're shy, modest, introverted. We don't know how others will react to what we say, so we don't say anything, or say something different from what we mean.

But you know what? The sky won't crack, the world won't stop spinning, and your half second won't get any shorter or longer if you share your goals with others. *Try it.* You'll be pleasantly surprised – uplifted, empowered by the act of letting others know you have plans, that you're going places. *So speak.* Hearing yourself say that you're going to do something carries weight, conviction. It's a mega bomb more powerful than just writing it,

---

30 Matthews, G. Study Backs up Strategy for Achieving Goals, Dominican University of California, 2010

which in turn is a mega bomb more powerful than just thinking it.

Speak!

Define it, write it, say it – say it out loud! Liberate your unspoken dreams, bring them to life, give them wings. Whatever you believe in, whether you think there's an afterlife or not, whether your soul flies to heaven or dissolves into the dirt, one thing is certain: *You will never be you again* – in this day and age, there will never be another *you.* This is your one and only life, all half second of it, so make the most of it. Get what you want. See, do, feel everything you've dreamed of seeing, doing, feeling. If you've ever had a dream, if you've ever gazed at the stardust flung across the night sky and wondered "how do I get there? – *how do others get there?*" now is the time to change your direction, now is the time to chart a new course for *there.*

Action Items

In the half second we call life, few of us ever sit down and think, *Where am I? How did I get here? Where am I going? Is that where I want to go?* At work, we take time out for "strategy sessions." We review the business, its performance, customers, position in the marketplace. We consider the future and create all sorts of plans and goals. And yet, when it comes to something infinitely more important than work – *our life* – we don't have time. There's too much going on to have a strategy session, to make plans, set goals. We become a passenger and take the road as it comes, speed bumps, potholes, and all.

But now is the time to make time. Now is the time to sit down and ask yourself those questions; now is the time to frame the answers as goals. *Take control of your life.* Make it into what you want – millions have done so already, and there's no reason you can't as well. *Your half second is ticking.*

To walk through the first door of success:

- *Define your goals*. Create a few one-year goals and a giant three-year goal. The one-year goals should be within reach, such as increased savings, promotion, education, more time with loved ones, weight loss. But the three-year goal should be dramatic, something that is not readily within reach, like financial independence, starting a business, or making a sea change.

- *Make your goals precise.* You already have the element of "time" in your goals represented by a number (one year and three years), and now add more numbers (percentages, units, pounds, dollars) and/or concrete events and milestones (university degree, starting your own business, becoming a parent). Even if you have many goals across work, family, health, and hobbies, each goal should be as sharp and unambiguous as a razor's edge.

- *Visualize your goals.* When you're falling asleep at night, don't think about the problems of the day or what you saw on television. Instead, visualize your goals. See them, feel them, touch them. This provides your mind with additional focus and clarity about the goals you've set.

- *Share your goals with family and friends.* This may be awkward at first, but it will strengthen your commitment. When friends and family ask what you're up to, tell them about your goals. *Speak!*

Remember that everything is created twice: *first in the mind, then in reality*. The Door of Clarity is about the first creation, in your mind – a sharp, vivid picture of your goals and the kind of life you want to design for yourself. Without clarity, success is impossible, accidental. You won't achieve success if you don't know what success is.

"I would rather be ashes than dust."
Jack London

The Second Door

Jud Bowman is one of my favorite entrepreneurs. In high school, at the age of eighteen, he developed a prototype for contextual search on a mobile phone. Eager to commercialize his invention in the dot-com craze of the late 1990s, he flew to Silicon Valley right after graduation and pounded Sand Hill Road in search of investors. Most people listened to him with parental sympathy before showing him the door. He suffered rejection after rejection after rejection; 57 times he was told "no." Dejected, beaten down, he was about to call it quits and head back home, when a little miracle happened. An investor – impressed by the kid from nowhere who wouldn't take no for an answer – threw some money at Jud's idea to see what would happen.

A lot happened.

Jud developed his prototype further and, with the

investor's help, co-founded a company called *Pinpoint Networks*. In the years that followed, *Pinpoint Networks* became *Motricity*, growing to almost $150 million in revenue and 500 employees. The company went public on the stock market in 2010, and at its peak, enjoyed a market value of more than one *billion* dollars.

Like I said, Jud is one of my favorite entrepreneurs.

In his early days, when he was running Pinpoint Networks, we both lived in the same state, both ran venture capital-backed technology companies, and both enjoyed the energy and enthusiasm of youth. It didn't take us long to meet. And when I moved to Australia many years later, I asked Jud to fly out and share his success story with local entrepreneurs. He graciously agreed.

By the time he arrived, we hadn't seen each other in a long while; I was onto my next business and he was reaching the peak of his days at Motricity. We met for dinner at my favorite steak house, and over several bottles of crimson wine, Jud related his latest exploits back home. Carl Ichan, the billionaire investor and legendary corporate raider, had invested a mind-numbing $100 million into Motricity. They were going public soon; the stock would be worth *billions*. And Jud would be ringing the stock exchange bell on their first day of trading.

With words as brushstrokes, he painted the landscape of mobile technology and how the future would unfold. Google was releasing Android, the Apple iPhone was storming the market, and people in India and China were enjoying their first internet experience on a mobile device rather than a personal computer. Jud had met with the Google founders to discuss it. Customers across the globe were waiting with bated breath and Silicon Valley was abuzz.

As Jud continued to speak, excitement raced through my veins, fire-like. My temperature rose and the room began to sway. And through it all, through the haze and fog and blurring heat, an unexpected idea presented itself. *What the hell am I doing here?* I thought. *I could be ringing that bell on the stock exchange, it could be me.* I had the skills, contacts, the means. *All I had to do was return to the United States, get my old team back, raise a few million dollars, jump back into the tech game.* It would be like old times, when I sat at tables with Fortune 500 CEOs and former heads of state. *I did it before, I could do it again.* I felt my hand on the bell – smooth, glossy, clear as daybreak. *All I had to do was ring it.*

I looked up – Jud's lips were moving, but I wasn't listening. My thoughts were stepping out in front of me, onto the street, towering from the streetlamp to the fringes of outer space. Visions appeared and danced and then went backstage, before coming back for encores. The stock market bell kept ringing. *Ding! Ding! Ding! Ding! Ding! Ding! Ding! Ding!* I couldn't make it stop. I was on a 747 space-bound for the moon. I wanted to pack my suitcase and get going. *What was I waiting for? When was the next flight out of Australia?*

The wine grew bolder, more audacious. A procession of elephants sauntered through the room, in pairs, wearing gold-plated saddles that sparkled with precious stones. Fireworks boomed overhead as jugglers and clowns skipped through the street, blowing flames into the air. A magician pulled an airplane ticket from his hat while a team of illusionists made the city disappear.

Nothing was impossible, everything was within reach.

When it was time to leave, when we finally stumbled out of the restaurant onto the street, the air hit my face like desert wind blown over a thousand miles of burning sand. It was the middle of winter, people were dressed up, yet I was standing in an oven, a humid, feverish inferno. My face was wet, flush; my shirt clinging to my shoulders like plastic wrap on a bowl of leftovers. I could feel the bell in one hand and the door of the taxicab in the other.

But as we parted ways, as I fell into the taxi and waited to arrive at my front door, my excitement began to cool. The flashing lights and colors of the city fell away. It grew quiet. The air turned cold and pulled the heat from my face. And as the taxi floated through darkness, the raw and rampant visions of yester-minute weakened and became less grand. When I finally arrived at home, I found my wife and kids waiting for me. My two boys flew across the room like sparrows, into my arms, their tiny fingers and thumbs tugging at my collar. My heart grew soft and melted. The last of my thoughts and visions, peering barefaced from the shadows, dissolved into the nothingness from which they had emerged.

I was home. Not in airports or airplanes, not in boardrooms or boozy meetings, but home, with them, where I belonged – *where I wanted to be above all else.* As I pulled the scent of their baby skin into my lungs, deeply and purposefully, the bell slipped from my fingers. I knew I wouldn't return to the United States, or get my old team back, or raise millions of dollars, or get back into the Silicon Valley tech game. Something had changed; something was different. *That something was me.*

How Much You Want It

Have you ever wondered why you do what you do? Why you're willing to labor and sacrifice for some goals, but not others? Why you exercise and eat healthy or not bother at all? Have you ever wondered what drives your decisions and goals? What makes you go left in life rather than right?

Desire.

As raw and primordial as the caveman himself, desire sits behind all your actions; *desire is the reason you do what you do.* You may not enjoy your job, you may not enjoy exercising – you may even hate it – but you intensely desire your paycheck and staying fit, so much so that you're willing to struggle through work and working out, day in, day out, for the outcome. That's desire, running in the background, influencing your every decision.

Desire is the second door of success.

Philosophers have been philosophizing over desire for centuries, some crediting it as the fundamental driver of all human action.[31] I share this view. No matter how big or small, I believe that *all* our decisions stem from desire, from how much we *want* something. Take dieting. It's quite straightforward to lose weight – just restrict food and start exercising. Anyone can do it. And yet, few people succeed because dieting is "uncomfortable." Hunger pangs, dizzy spells, mood swings, cravings, headaches, and more frustrate our efforts. Most people prefer a full belly to an empty one, the couch over the treadmill. So why do some succeed in losing weight, while others fail?

One reason: *desire.* Some people *want* it more.

If your desire to lose weight (with all its discomforts) exceeds your desire to maintain the status quo (of favorite foods and no exercise), then you'll take action and diet. If it doesn't, you'll do nothing; you'll maintain the status quo. It's really that simple. And sticking to your diet for months on end – something people call *persistence* – is really nothing more than your desire

---

31 Most notably, Thomas Hobbes (1588–1678), best known for his work on political philosophy and social contracts. His view of human nature was that people's actions are determined solely by their individual desires and aversions (Leviathan, 1651)

staying strong. *Week in, week out, you want it as badly as the day you started.*

If you abandon your diet midstream, it means your desire for food, alcohol, time away from the treadmill, overpowered your desire to lose weight. The diet failed because you succumbed to a greater desire. At the very moment of failure, as you binged on feel-good foods, your desire for satiety exceeded all other desires, even losing weight. Had you really wanted to lose weight – had your desire for weight loss remained strong – you would have stayed on the diet. Despite all the excuses and explanations, that's the real reason.

You can try to fool yourself and insist that you don't *desire* to lose weight; you *must* lose weight for health reasons. You don't want to, but you *must.* But there is no "must" in life – only choice, freewill. Your desire to avoid health problems is greater than your desire to maintain the status quo. So you *choose* to lose weight. Again, desire drives your decision.

No matter how far you branch out, all your decisions will still come back to the same root: *desire.* Even things you detest doing, you do them for some desirable outcome, such as pleasing your parents, spouse, receiving a pay-check, avoiding health problems, and so on. In fact, in *all* the things you've ever done, you've either enjoyed doing them or you've desired the outcome (or both). Otherwise, there would be no logical reason to do them.

Books and experts have debated the subject of desire to no end. In the process, they've tossed around *motivation, ambition, persistence, drive,* and *perseverance* like so much salad. To achieve goals you must "motivate yourself," "be persistent," "stay driven," and so on, ad nauseam, until reflux occurs and the half-digested salad comes back up. I want you to forget all those words. They confuse and complicate that which is clear and simple. If you're studying psychology, behaviorism, if you're doing a PhD in higher education, or becoming a philosopher, go ahead and expand your vocabulary. But if you're here, on this page, to unlock success rather than diplomas, forget everything save *desire.* All other terms are superfluous. Either you desire X more than Y, or Y more than X. In either case, your decision is determined by what you desire most.

Desire and goals

A considerable body of research supports the view that you're *far* more likely to achieve goals you desire than goals you don't.[32] *Why?* Because desire creates commitment,

---

32 Atkinson, J.W. "Motivational determinants of risk taking behavior," *Psychological Review*, 1957; Vroom, V.H. *Work and Motivation,* Wiley, 1964; Brehm, J.W., & Self, E. "The intensity of motivation," Annual Review of Psychology, 1987; Locke, E.A. & Latham, G.P. *A Theory of Goal Setting and Task Performance,* Prentice Hall, 1990; Ajzen, I. *The theory of Planned Behavior, Organizational Behavior and Human Decision Processes,* 1991; Bandura, A. *Self-efficacy: The exercise of control,* Freeman, 1997; Carver, C.S., & Scheier, M.F. *On the Self-regulation of Behavior,* Cambridge University Press, 1998; and Waitley, D., *Psychology of Success,* McGraw-Hill, 2010

helps you overcome obstacles, and helps you recover from setbacks and disappointments, and keeps you going. You must have desire for the goals you've set. Without it, you'll fail. No matter how precise your goals are, no matter how vivid and clear, you won't achieve them without desire. Period.

Do you know why some people achieve astonishing success while others look on with envy? Why some people set sporting records, build multi-million-dollar companies, file patents for inventions, write books and poems, make scientific breakthroughs, while others watch? It's because they desire their goals with an intensity akin to fervor, obsession. *That is the secret.* Their desire is a passion, like being madly in love.

Have you ever been madly in love?

Have you ever felt desire for another person that was so consuming, so overwhelming, that you could hear the fabric of your soul tearing? *That is real desire.* That's the emotion that enables extraordinary success – that keeps the body going, forward, uphill, against the probabilities, in the face of long odds, to achieve, to succeed. For those looking on from the outside, they see *motivation, ambition, drive.* But on the inside, in the soul, there is only *desire*; stronger than hunger, drier than thirst, it punches ahead with a "can't-live-without-it" force. If you desire your goals with such fervor, you will succeed – *I promise you will succeed.*

When I met up with Jud Bowman in Australia, all those years ago, I realized that my desire to be a great parent outweighed my desire to get back to Silicon Valley. I knew "Cat's in the Cradle" by heart.[33] I knew its lesson. My success would be empty, hollow, if my kids grew up without me – if they related to "Cat's in the Cradle" and felt that it described their life. The greatest financial success would be ash in my mouth. And as this realization descended upon me, I knew the grand visions of the United States, Silicon Valley, stock market bells, and plenty more, were visions that were destined to remain visions. No matter how clearly I saw them, no matter how precisely I defined them as goals, *the desire to chase them had been overtaken by an even greater desire.*

Alignment

Have you ever wondered what the odds of success are? The likelihood of achieving your goals? Then measure your desire – that's the answer, that's the probability of success. The more you desire something, the more likely you are to achieve it. Why? Because desire will force you to think about your goals – *it will be difficult to think of anything else.* And the more you think about your goals, the

---

33 "Cat's in the Cradle" is a 1974 pop song by Harry Chapin from the album Verities & Balderdash. The single topped the Billboard Hot 100 in December 1974.

more focused your mind will get, the clearer your goals will become, and the more effort you'll put into achieving them. You're far more likely to succeed in such state of mind, which is why desire heavily influences your probability of success.

For this reason, there's no point in setting goals you don't truly desire. These are the wrong goals for you, and you're unlikely to achieve them. You may write down a goal of losing twenty pounds of fat over a six-month period. It's a precise goal, like vanilla yogurt on aisle four. But what if you neatly fold that piece of paper in half, and place it at the back of your desk drawer? And what if months pass, exercise becomes an afterthought, and your daily fare consists of fish and chips followed by ice-cream? It's obvious that your desire to lose twenty pounds is low; in all likelihood, you've probably forgotten all about it. Losing weight was a wish, something nice-to-have, and such goals are seldom achieved.[34]

On the work front, you may set a goal of securing a promotion before the year runs out. Again, it's a clear goal and one that's easy to visualize. But after setting the goal, what if you come to work late, leave early, miss important meetings, and hand in sloppy reports? What does that mean? One thing: that your desire for the goal

---

34 Most people experience a crisis (such as health problems or being unable to fit into a normal chair) before their desire for weight loss reaches a critical threshold and they get serious about exercise and diet

is low. It means you don't really care about the promotion and won't be bothered if you miss it. Again, this is the wrong goal for you.

The thought of not achieving your goal *must* bother you. In fact, the more it bothers you, *the better*; it means your desire is high. It bothers me tremendously to think of failing in my goal of being there for my kids – of really being *there*, for soccer games, school functions, birthdays, the lot. Because the thought of failure is so harsh, like a steel grater on my heart, the desire to achieve this personal goal is immense. And for that very simple and straightforward reason – *because my desire is so high* – I'm likely to succeed.

The key to the Door of Desire is to *align your goals with desire*.

Five things you hate

For most people, aligning goals and desire is easier said than done. We may feel lost, unsure of what we want, or torn between conflicting emotions and directions. We might be unable to relate to the intense desire that success legends like Richard Branson, Arnold Schwarzenegger, or Steve Jobs exhibited during their rise – we simply don't have the same heat or sense of urgency. We may read *The Alchemist*,[35] put the book down and not know what our personal legend is, or if we even have one. Not

---

35 International best-selling novel by Paulo Coelho, first published in Brazil, 1988

everyone knows their heart so well they can rattle off their deepest desires without blinking.

But the process of aligning your goals and desire doesn't have to be messy or mysterious; there are a number of exercises you can employ. One of my favorites is writing down the five most *negative* things in your life – that's right, the five things you hate most about your life. These negatives typically relate to work, personal finance, relationships, appearance, or living conditions. Once you've identified these items, compare them to your goals. Are your goals aligned to the list? Do your goals directly address the negative forces in your life? If so, you have alignment. Your desire to change these negatives will be high, and for that reason, the probability of achieving your goals will also be high.*

Imagine that one of your goals is to find a better-paying job. You then complete this exercise, and at the very top of your list of negatives is your monthly battle to cover rent and living expenses, and your boss at work who doesn't like you. Your goal of finding a better-paying job is strongly aligned to the negatives in your life. Your desire to remove these negatives will be high, and consequently, your desire to achieve the goal will also be high. Your goals and desire are aligned.

---

* The same approach can also be used in business, where you list the five most negative aspects of your company or division (such as market share, revenue, net profit, customer service, employer turnover, product innovation, etc.) and align your business goals to address these negatives.

In completing this exercise, it should be easier to list the things you *don't want* in your life, than the things you *do want*. Why? Because the things you don't want already exist. You don't have to imagine them. They are already part of your life, in plain sight. Pay attention to how you feel about them. They should trigger more emotion than any theoretical goal. Your negatives are real, you're living with them right now, *and they bother you!* The anger, frustration, despair you feel is *desire* – desire for change! If you live in the ghetto, with gangs and drugs and guns, your environment might be the most negative aspect of your life. If so, your desire to move will be high, and you'll aggressively pursue any goal aligned to this desire. But your move depends entirely on whether you view living in the ghetto as a negative. If you're the leader of a gang and benefit from the environment, then you might view the ghetto as a positive rather than negative. And if that's the case, any goal to move would be pointless and not aligned to your desire.

Many of our most powerful desires and goals stem from the negative forces in our lives. Most people want to get rich not for the sake of being rich, but because they want to quit their job and do something else before their half second runs out. Their desire for wealth stems from the powerful realization that they're doing what they "have to" in life – work, eat, pay bills – rather than what they "want to." This negative fuels their desire for wealth, money, and freedom.

Scoring your desire

Another way of aligning your goals and desire is by assigning a "desire score" to your goals. "10" for must-have goals, where the thought of failure is unbearable, and "1" for nice-to-have goals, where failure doesn't bother you one bit. The higher your desire score, the greater the probability you'll achieve the goal. And the bigger your goals, the more desire you'll need to achieve them.

When you step out of small goals, like financial buffers against the unexpected, and step into life-changing goals, like financial independence, your desire must be 10+, off the scale. It can no longer be a vague sensation in your gut that squeals incoherently, a sensation so calm and tranquil it almost goes unnoticed. When it comes to the big things in life, to scaling mountains and slaying dragons, your desire must be as hot as the sun, nuclear, an emotion so intense it prevents sleep and keeps you yearning for the break of dawn.

In the context of goals, desire is your *fuel*. The larger your goal, the more fuel you'll need to get there. By assigning a desire score to each of your goals, you can see if you've got enough fuel to get there.

Dreambox

The most powerful way of aligning your goals and desire is through your heart. All the great achievers of the ages have done this. Their desire to achieve greatness was beyond fire, hotter than volcanos and exploding stars – *their desire was destiny. They did what they were meant to do.*

Such greatness begins in childhood, when our minds are free of limits and boundaries. Dreams of becoming an astronaut, race-car driver, movie star – roaring to the moon, across the track, under strobe lights – are all within reach. We put all of these dreams into a box, a *dreambox*. No dream is too large for our box; anything can fit in there. And each day we open the box and play with our dreams, like so many dolls, imagining the day they'll become true.

Then adolescence comes. We change, begin to see things differently, and we change some of our dreams. We know the world a little better now; we know who we are, what we like, what interests us. We replace some of our dreams with new ones, and our hearts race when we think of tomorrow.

The future is bright.

But then the seasons roll forward, and we're flung out of school and into life with the force of a catapult. Months pass with breakneck speed, like falling down stairs. We don't open our dreambox as much; we don't have time.

We celebrate New Year's Day, and before we can wipe the glitter from our eyes, we're celebrating it again, and again. We walk down the street, turn a corner, and our footsteps multiply as we find ourselves with spouses, kids, responsibilities, mortgages, bills, worries. We stop looking inside our dreambox. *It hurts to look inside.* The gap between our dreams and reality is yawning wide. *Foolish youth*, we think.

And then one day, we open our dreambox for the last time. The gap is now a gulf, insurmountable, hopeless. We close the lid and have a midlife crisis. Our dreams of youth – always there, in the background, providing hope and encouragement – are no more. We look in the mirror. We're too old, too tired, too committed, too overextended. We close the dreambox and throw it away.

Deep lines spider our face, our eyes harden, we forget our dreambox ever existed. We become a machine of routine, living always in the present, one day to the next, hoping only that nothing breaks. We no longer dream; *we* no longer know what a dream is. One day our children ask us about dreams and we struggle to answer; we don't know, we can't think in such paradigms anymore. We're locked into routine – into breakfast, work, dinner, family, TV, bed – and can only experience incremental thought. Our life has become a movie, a drama that onlookers philosophize over. The kind of movie you see every day, in every town and city around the world, playing over and over and over, stuck in replay.

The coalminers

The agonizing defeat of our dreams and desires reminds me of an interview that took place some decades ago between a West European journalist and several East European coalminers. The session began with the journalist asking about their families and background. The miners went into some detail, notwithstanding the discomfort of their helmets, harnesses, and cramped quarters of the squat room. The journalist then asked what they would most like to change about their lives. From the chasms of the ocean to the craters of the moon, the question was without limit. The miners looked at the journalist and then at each other.

"Anything?" one of them ventured to asked.

"Anything at all," the journalist replied, pen hanging over paper.

The miner cleared his throat. "Well, I take two trains to work, and the connection between them is an hour," he explained, pausing, hesitating, intimidated by the sheer magnitude of his desire. After a brief silence he took a deep breath and made the big wish, as if his existence depended on it: *"I wish the connection was only five minutes."*

The words seemed to hang in the air, oppressive, suffocating, worse than fallout. The journalist opened his mouth to speak but a groan accidentally slipped out instead. It sounded so forlorn and defeated that the miners looked at the ceiling, believing his soul had escaped to heaven. They stared, like owls peering through masks of soot, and waited. The journalist saw the coaldust ingrained in their flesh, an indelible tattoo of work and toil. He saw hard labor in their eyes – labor and nothing but labor, as routine without hope or reprieve. The silence finally ended with the sound of his notebook closing. He didn't have any more questions.

I sometimes wonder if we're like those coalminers? *Trapped, underground, darkness without dreams.* On the outside, we are unrecognizably different. Gadgets rather than helmets, scented lotion instead of coaldust, designer brands in lieu of harnesses. But on the inside, under the tinsel and hype, are we really that different? Are we ever pulling at the stars, tugging, reaching, promising we'll be there soon? Or are we resigned to life, fate, the way things are? It seems the older we get, the more the routine of life has us by the throat, our goals become smaller and more incremental – a promotion, home renovation, overseas vacation, better car. In the case of the coalminers, their routine was so entrenched, so absolute, that changing their morning commute became a dream of the highest magnitude.

I believe that deep down inside, deeper than we let anyone go, even ourselves, we desire something larger than the incremental change of a promotion, new car, or overseas vacation. *We desire something from our dreambox.* If we were king for a day or could wish upon a star, our real goal might be to start a business, change careers, sail around the world, move to another country, pursue our true love. But we can't face our family or ourselves with such goals. So our desires remain repressed and unspoken, wrapped in blankets in the basement of our subconscious, and we go through life setting goals that are small and incremental. Our desire for these goals is not great, but neither are the goals.

Your deepest desires, your hottest fires, are in your dreambox. It's where you'll find your big dreams. It's where you'll find sparks, pulsating stars, the roar of splitting atoms. *It's where you'll find your heart.* If you align your goals to what's in your dreambox, you'll experience a feeling of destiny, of unity with the cosmos – an inexplicable conviction that everything is "right" because you're doing exactly what you're supposed to be doing. Talk to any person who has achieved extraordinary success, and you'll hear them describe this feeling; they all have it.

If you look at the soul-stirring art on cathedral ceilings, you can almost see the painters on their back, centuries ago, brushing their soul into each stroke, and understand them. Tired and thirsty, muscles cramping, exhausted, blind from plaster and stone, they cannot stop. Desire has them; it's destiny – a dream from their dreambox. That's the feeling those who succeed have. They're on a mission, a higher calling. And it's because their oversized goals are straight from their dreambox. They never close the lid; they live in it, with it, always.

You can achieve your greatest potential if your goals align with what's inside your dreambox. No matter how large the gulf, no matter how harsh the contrast, I encourage you to find your dreambox and open it. It may hurt, make your eyes wet, squeeze your heart, bring you to crisis, but if you don't, your life will never feel "right." You'll forever be haunted by a vague sadness, deep beneath the surface, a pea under a thousand mattresses, a feeling that things could've been different, that you never really made the most of life, that somewhere along the way you made the wrong decision, set the wrong goals, *that you missed your destiny in life.*

Opening your dreambox

Career psychologists attempt to access people's dreams by asking questions such as, *What would you do if money didn't matter? What goals would you set if you had $10 million in the bank?* But this approach lacks realism. Most people worry about money on a regular basis, so asking them about goals they would set if money didn't matter is too far removed from their real-life situation. Another approach used by career psychologists is to explore our childhood dreams. But this approach also lacks realism, as few of us would want to pursue the dreams we had at the age of six – our dreams change.

But there's a better way of approaching this exercise. I believe that people abandon their dreams because of the risks and consequences of failure. That's the over-powering negative force that holds them back. If you hypothetically remove this negative by asking, *What would you do if you couldn't fail? If success was guaranteed?* your dreambox will suddenly become more accessible. Such questions touch upon the deepest desires you have *today* – not the ones you had yesterday, or the ones you might have in the future – but the ones you have right now. And those are the only ones that matter. Try it, I dare you: *What would you do if you couldn't fail?*

You may have guessed that this book is from my dreambox; it's been there a long time. But the desire to write it also stems from the greatest negative in my life, my deepest secret, *the inescapable feeling that my life is insignificant.* It's a spur in my soul, always there, a reminder that I have less "days left" today than I did yesterday; that my half second will be over soon, too soon, before I'm ready, and I need to do something significant before the end comes. This negative tops my list.

So what can I do?

Create something that will survive me, live beyond the grave, after me. The idea first assailed me while reading Jack London's books. I wasn't winded by the strength of his style, or the truth and vigor he imprisoned with words; no, that wasn't it. I was winded by the realization that Jack London was reaching out to me, across space, time, death itself, to influence my life, to make me see the world in a different way. And I knew, at that very moment, that I had to write – that writing was the greatest thing in the world.

And so here I am today, tomorrow, yesterday, pounding the keys with fire in my heart, waging war to free my thoughts. I am feverish. I cannot sleep. I cannot wait for the sun to break to continue writing, in haste, against time, against the vanishing day, letting emotion pour forth like dams breaking. And the whole while, as my fingertips gallop across the keyboard, I have this all-pervading feeling of rightness – that everything has never been more *right*.

Constant Change

Everything changes. The weather, economy, medicine, technology, knowledge, political leaders – *everything*. In the same way that leaves fade, fall, grow, in circles, without rest or end, our lives are defined by change. We change cars, houses, jobs, careers; we move from infancy to adolescence to midlife and beyond; we watch loved ones enter and leave the world; we see change around us, in us, everywhere, and realize one day that everything is in flux, never steady. And because life has so many moving pieces, we tend to wait for things to slow down before setting goals and making plans. *We wait for the right time.* And wait. Decades pass, and … you know the rest. But there's no point in waiting. The *only* constant in life is change. Don't be afraid to set goals because there's change in your life; stop waiting for the "right time." There's no such thing as the right time, it doesn't exist. The only time that matters is *now* – your half second is ticking.

However well you align your goals and desire, whether it's through identifying the negatives in your life or opening your dreambox, that alignment will break down sooner or later. As your life changes, as *you* change, your dreams and desires will also change. *And that's okay* – that's life. That's the way of the world. You must embrace this process, and when significant change occurs, you must realign your goals and desire. Let desire guide you – there's no other test or method. If you're still on fire to achieve your goals, then keep them. *They're still the right goals.* But if your desire changes, then your goals must also change. You must always strive for alignment.

For some reason, people believe that goals must be set in stone, cemented into eternity, never to be changed or modified. They assume that "permanence" creates commitment, thereby making goals easier to achieve. But this type of thinking puts people off from setting goals in the first place. *There's just too much going on right now*, they think. *I can't possibly plan that far ahead.* And so they wait, and wait, for the right time.

But dreams and goals are not static; they change as your life changes. So there's no point in contemplating how you might feel, who you might be, what you might want in the future. Nobody knows what the future may bring – not you, not me, nobody. The only thing that matters is your desire *now*, what you're willing to work for, struggle for, *now*. Once you get *there*, you can re-evaluate your desire and realign your goals. Trust your desire to guide you in this process. You cannot change what you desire in the same way you cannot change your height or skin color. You are who you are, and your desire is what it is.

Follow it!

Action items

You've defined your goals, made them precise through the use of dates, dollars and other numbers. You've committed them to paper. You've shared them with friends and family. *So far so good.* You are firmly through the Door of Clarity. You know exactly what you want.

So what's next?

The second door of success: *Desire.* It will determine whether you achieve your goals or fall short. Without desire, there's no commitment, there's nothing to push you, pull you, when you've got nothing left to push and pull with. Without desire, success is impossible. And like the low-carb diet, the Door of Desire only has one rule: *the greater your desire, the greater your probability of success.*

To walk through the second door of success:

■ *Align your goals with your desire.* Use a combination of methods, from identifying the negatives in your life, through to desire scores and your dreambox. Then go back to your one-year and three-year goals. Do you have alignment? How many "10"s do you have? Is your desire fiery, irrepressible, aching to erupt with the force of a thousand volcanoes spewing lava? Or it is tepid, sleepy, like moss in the shade? The objective of this exercise is to modify your goals so they align to your strongest desires. You stand the greatest chance of achieving success if all your goals are "must-have" goals, where life isn't worth living without them. *You must have alignment.*

■ *Write a letter to yourself from the future.* That's right, you read that correctly – write a letter to yourself from the future. Describe what your life looks like after achieving your goals. From waking up in the morning to going to bed at night, describe what you do, see, hear, and feel. If your goals include weight loss, describe your new clothes, the lightness of your step, what you're eating, how you're training, the compliments you're getting through looks and glances – *write it!* Whatever it is – a new job, car, career, relationship – write a letter from the future about it, about having it, about what success tastes like. To make the exercise easier, write two letters: the first from one year in the future, after you've achieved your one-year goals, and the second from three years in the future. In the letter, *remember that you've already achieved your goals.* This is critical. You must explain, in the greatest detail, what life looks like with the goals behind you, done.

The "letter from the future" is a particularly interesting and useful exercise because it forces your mind into the future. You have to visualize all the particulars of what success looks like, *you have to create the future in your mind.* This brings your clarity to new heights, as a "day in your future life" demands more detail than a two-sentence goal. This is also another test for aligning your goals and desire. If it's a chore to write these letters, to describe what your life looks like in the future, then chances are you still don't have alignment. You should be jumping out of your skin to describe the accomplishment of your goals. It should be the most exciting thing in the world.

You must have desire!

"Do or do not ... there is no try."
Yoda

The Third Door

*Y**ou're special. You can do anything, be anyone,* my parents always told me. It felt good to hear, and I heard it often while growing up. Somewhere along the way, it sunk in, fused with my psyche, and became me.

With such state of mind, at the age of fourteen, I opened Arnold Schwarzenegger's *Encyclopaedia of Modern Bodybuilding*. It was a tome, a thousand pages long, a forearm workout in itself. I read it cover-to-cover and gaped at the pictures with a sense of religious awe. Muscles, strength, *respect.* I wanted to look like *that.* I was in high school now, and muscles mattered in high school. I took Arnold's book and cut it to pieces, carefully pulling the best pictures from the pages and onto the walls and mirrors of my parents' house. And there they stood, the best bodybuilders of my time, tanned, immortal, skin as thin as paper, muscle on top of muscle built by years of damning toil, covered in veins, spider-like, rippling and quivering beneath sheets of taut skin.

I looked at the pictures and then at myself. White, smooth, like a melted marshmallow. I flexed my arm – nothing. I searched for my six-pack but only found jelly-rolls. I flexed my upper leg, calves, triceps. Sweat rolled down my back. I hit a side chest pose. My face turned red. I tried looking for my six-pack again but I was all out of breath. I had only managed to catch a dimple here and there, nothing more. My muscles were trapped under years of corn syrup. I took my measurements: 12-inch arm, 36 waist, 152 pounds. I looked at the pictures again, then back at myself. The contrast between Arnold's 22-inch arm and my 12-inch reflection hurt. I was soft, small, weak.

The gulf between the pictures and my reflection seemed to widen, but faster than it widened, soared my desire to close it. *What those bodybuilders had done, I could do.* The frown on my face receded. *I could do anything, be anyone* – my parents had told me so. And besides, Arnold had provided me with a step-by-step formula for success. I couldn't lose. I read the pictureless, shredded fragments of his book again. I found his formula. I memorized it. All I had to do was train four hours a day, six days a week, sleep in the sun, eat a dozen eggs, two pounds of meat, gallon of milk, and I would succeed. I would even make millions of dollars, just like Arnold.

My desire raged. I joined a gym and began working out. I jogged in the morning, went to school during the day, and lifted weights in the evening. I changed my diet, took my measurements each week, and watched my body morph. My waist shrank, 36, 35, 34, 33, 32, 31, and finally 30. My weight dropped to 130 pounds as the fat fell off, and then climbed back 135, 140, 145, 150, 155, as muscle filled my frame. My arms stretched the tape from 12 to 15 inches. My parents bought me new clothes and I felt the tightness in my wardrobe move from waist to shoulders. My frown disappeared and never came back. I was off on my journey, in orbit, outer space.

I set monthly goals for size and strength – 10 pounds on this lift, 5 pounds on that; a ¼ inch here, a ¼ inch there. I willed the tape to stretch. I visualized it, fantasized about it, morning, night, and each minute in between. More pictures appeared on my mirror. Bodybuilding books began to line my bedroom wall. I trained longer, harder. My arms crossed over 16 inches, my weight swelled to 175. I began tanning on weekends and my skin lost its ghost-white sheen. Even my face changed. My cheekbones stood out and wiggly veins appeared on my temples. My eyes moved back, deeper and bluer than before. I was no longer soft.

But I wanted more.

My desire continued to rage. I wanted to walk into the pictures on my mirror. I stormed the public library for books and magazines, stressing my eyes late into the night reading about diet and nutrition. I studied the protocols of other bodybuilders and began to track my progress in a training diary. *I could get there*, I kept telling myself. *My parents had told me so.* But my parents had doubts about where my life was heading. I had forgotten about college and career; nothing mattered save chalk dust and the bang and clang of iron plates. And so they sat me down one evening, very serious-like, and asked about the future.

"Have you given much thought about college?" my father asked. "And what you're interested in – what you'll major in?" my mother added.

There was chalk dust everywhere; I tried waving it away, but it got stuck in my throat. "College? Major?" I couldn't stop blinking. "Actually, you know, I thought about *not* going to college."

The color drained from their faces. They coughed. "But why? What would you do instead?"

"Bodybuilding."

"*Bodybuilding?*" The chalk dust seemed to be choking them as well. "But how will you *live?* How will you support yourself?"

My face lit up; the path to success burned bright in my mind. It was so simple, I told them. I'd train four hours a day, sleep in the sun, eat a dozen eggs, two pounds of meat, gallon of milk, and make millions of dollars – just like Arnold. "I don't have time for college," I concluded. "It would cut into my training."

My parents didn't reply for a while. They just sat there. Thinking. Anxiety and worry stamped into their eyes and hearts. I waited for their response: the arguments, the logic, all the reasons why I should change direction. But I waited in vain. Instead of fighting me head on, my parents took a different approach.

"Son," my father began, better than a lawyer preparing for the close. "We want you to pursue your dreams and we think you'll succeed in whatever you do – *you know that*. But wouldn't it be smart to have *a backup plan*? You know, *just in case*."

They had my attention; I was listening. "What kind of *backup plan*?"

"Enrol at the university for one class per semester," they explained, reaching the pivotal point of their argument. "You'll be officially enrolled and studying toward a degree. Then – *God forbid!* – should you fail to become the next Arnold, you can simply increase your class load, finish your degree, and have ..." he paused, struggling for the right word, "... a *normal* life. You'll have a *backup* plan to fall back on – you know, *just in case*."

Their advice resonated with me, and months later, I graduated from high school and enrolled for one class at the university. There was peace at home. But in my heart, I gave bodybuilding my all. I changed gyms to train with the best bodybuilders in town, and I trained like never before. Each moment at the gym was a torment, misery, as the pain cut and burned through my muscles, acid-like. But I grew. My arms pushed 17 inches; my weight jumped to 180, 185, and then 190. I lay in the sun almost every day, reading and studying, and developed a deep, golden tan in the process. Existence had never been so grand, like dice falling towards a perfect pair. *I could get there.* My parents had told me so.

But then another year passed, and something happened. I don't know what exactly – perhaps college took hold of my mind, just like my parents had hoped it would. Or I got tired of spending my days underneath a barbell. Or maybe I just grew up. Whatever it was, I was different, I had changed. I wasn't in high school anymore and muscles didn't mean what they used to. *Money did.* And I began to need it. I realized that no matter how big my shoulders got, I wouldn't get wealthy that way. I had been wrong about Arnold, about how he became wealthy. I read his biographies and found that his fortune came from business, not bodybuilding. First, it was mail order, then bricklaying, and finally real estate, where he made his first million.

My desire for financial freedom began to take hold. I saw the kind of life I wanted to have in the future; a life with someone I loved, with kids, living together in comfort, without stress or strain. And as such visions began to ferment, the yearning to become a champion bodybuilder waned. My desire no longer raged. I could get there – I *knew* I could get there – but I now wanted to go someplace different. And as I took the pictures down from my bathroom mirror, I looked back on my journey and smiled. I had come far. I had added 70 pounds of muscle to my frame in six years. I had learned self-discipline, to work through pain, to set goals. As I stared in the mirror, I remembered the melted marshmallow that used to stare back, and I felt a swell of inner power.

If I could achieve this, then I could achieve anything. There were no limits.

It was time to play catch-up at the university and I changed my major to something called "Finance." I rolled up my sleeves and got to work. And as I did so, I noticed my muscles dance and quiver underneath a thin layer of golden skin.

What You Believe

The well-documented *placebo effect*, where a patient's condition improves from using bogus medication, still defies our understanding of the connection between body and mind. Sugar pills have been the most consistent performer in clinical trials over the years, relieving pain, depression, disability, asthma, and other medical conditions as effectively as drugs and surgery.

Examples of this phenomenon abound.

Consider a double-blind study on asthma treatment, where patients given a fake inhaler reported identical asthma relief as those using a real inhaler.[36] Or patients in severe pain after wisdom tooth extraction who experienced equal relief from a fake application of ultrasound as another group who received the real thing.[37] And at the University of Rochester Medical Center, patients suffering from an inflammatory skin condition received either the prescription dose of steroid cream, or a fractional amount that was below the active dose of the drug and not enough to be effective. At the end of the study, both groups showed equal improvement and there was no difference in relapse.[38] The study broke new ground on the role of placebos in effective treatment.

But these examples pale in comparison to placebo studies that involve surgery. In one study involving 180 patients requiring knee surgery, some received the real treatment while others got a "sham operation." For the sham group, the whole routine was followed – getting

---

36 Wechsler, M.E., Kelley, J.M., Boyd, I.O, Dutile, S., Marigowda, G., Kirsch, I., Israel, E., Kaptchuk, T.J. "Active Albuterol or Placebo, Sham Acupuncture, or No Intervention in Asthma," *New England Journal of Medicine*, July 2011

37 Talbot, M. "The Placebo Prescription," *New York Times Magazine*, January 2000

38 Ader, R., Mercurio, M., Walton, J., James, D., Davis, M., Ojha, V., Kimball, A., Fiorentino, D. "Conditioned Pharmacotherapeutic Effects: A Preliminary Study," *Psychosomatic Medicine*, December 2009

wheeled into the operating theatre, preparation, anaesthesia, even making an incision in the knee – everything was real except that no actual surgery took place; the surgeon stitched the knee back up without doing anything. Of course, none of the patients knew. All of them believed they had undergone knee surgery.

The result?

Those who didn't get a real knee operation improved just as much as those that did.[39] One of patients in the sham group was in a wheelchair before the operation – he couldn't even walk. Weeks later, he was out playing basketball with his son in the backyard, a full recovery just like those who underwent the real operation. Despite the ethical questions that such studies raise, sham operations have also been carried out in place of brain surgery for Parkinson patients and spine surgery for patients suffering from cancer pain.[40]

If that's not remarkable enough, there's also the *nocebo effect*, which is the opposite of placebo. A nocebo is a harmless substance (just like a placebo) that creates harm in patients because they believe it's harmful – like getting an allergic reaction from a sugar pill because you

39 Moseley, J.B., O'Malley, K., Petersen, N.J., Menke, T.J., Brody, B.A., Kuykendall, D.H., Hollingsworth, J.C., Ashton, C.M., Wray, N.P. "A Controlled Trial of Arthroscopic Surgery for Osteoarthritis of the Knee," *New England Journal of Medicine*, July 2002

40 Stolberg, G., "Sham Surgery Returns as Research Tool," *New York Times*, 25 April, 1999

thought it was an antibiotic to which you're allergic. *Your mind created the allergic reaction, not the pill.*

One of the most powerful nocebo studies involved high school students who were allergic to lacquer trees (causing an itchy-rash reaction similar to poison ivy). The researcher blindfolded each student, rubbed a lacquer tree leaf on their arms, and told them not to worry, that it was just an ordinary leaf. Amazingly, their arm did not react, even though they were strongly allergic to lacquer trees. But the results get more amazing. The researcher then rubbed the other arm with an ordinary leaf, and again lied, telling each student it was a real lacquer tree leaf this time. Nothing should have happened, as an ordinary leaf was used but within minutes each student developed a red, bumpy rash.[41] Their physical reaction was not provoked by what *actually happened* – it was provoked by what they *believed had happened.* Their mind had created the response.

There's even a well-documented case where doctors incorrectly diagnosed a man with late-stage liver cancer, telling him he only had weeks or months to live. The man died a few months later, as predicted. But upon his autopsy, the misdiagnosis was discovered: there was no liver cancer. In fact, other than being dead, he was perfectly healthy.[42]

---

41 Morse, G., "The Nocebo Effect," *Hippocrates*, November 1999
42 "13 more things: The nocebo effect," *New Scientist*, 2 September 2009

What does all this mean? It means what you *believe* to be real is more important than what *is* real. It means you are defined by what you believe – that belief defines your reality.

Belief is the third door of success.

Now, don't get confused, I'm not talking about anything mystical or supernatural here. I'm not asking you to believe in any higher power, method, system, or technique for achieving success. You don't even have to believe in this book or anything I say. What you *must* believe in – and what I am talking about here – is believing in *yourself*.[43] How else can you possibly succeed? How can you succeed when, in your heart, you don't believe you can succeed? How is that supposed to work? How can you achieve your goals with such a mindset? And what are you expecting from success books? *Lotto numbers? Get-rich-quick schemes?*

Come on. Get real. You *must* believe in yourself. Self-belief is critical to success – even more critical than your actual capabilities. Studies have shown that your *belief* about your capabilities is a more accurate predictor of success than your *actual* capabilities.[44] Like the placebo and nocebo, *what you believe is more important than what is real.*

---

43 In psychology-speak, this belief is called "self-efficacy," which is your perceived capability to reach a goal (in contrast to your actual capability to reach a goal)

44 Bandura, A., "Perceived Self-Efficacy in Cognitive Development and Functioning," *Educational Psychologist*, April 1993

When I was bodybuilding, I didn't know much about genetics – of having long, full muscle bellies, narrow joints, evenly distributed body fat, thin skin, fast metabolism, and more. I never dreamed that some people could walk into a gym and make their muscles grow just by looking at the weights. I didn't have genes like that. In fact, I had just the opposite. I could walk into a grocery store and get fat just by looking at the candy bars. But I didn't know. No one told me. No one discouraged me. And because I didn't know about the shortcomings of my DNA, I grew, thrived, and succeeded. Had I known my limits, had I believed them, I would have been finished, done for. My belief would have limited my reality.

"Belief barriers"

One of the more famed stories about limits and self-belief is the four-minute mile. In all of history, nobody had ever run a mile in under four minutes. Nobody. For decades it loomed as a barrier, unbreakable, shatterproof. Benighted doctors said it couldn't be done, that the human body was incapable of running that fast, that it was dangerous to even try. We simply couldn't overcome our nature, our biomechanics.

Enter Roger Bannister. An Oxford student and gifted runner, he was weighing whether he should give up running after placing fourth at the 1952 Olympics. Instead, he decided to set himself a new goal: *to be the first man to run a mile in under four minutes.* He publicly announced his goal. His desire to succeed was high. He trained and trained and trained. On May 2nd 1953, he ran the mile in 4:03.6. Close. So close in fact, the attempt made him realize the four-minute mile was within reach. He believed he could do it. He continued to train. And a year later, on May 6th 1954, he recorded an official time of 3:59.4. His clear, crisp goal of being the first man to run the mile under four minutes was his, done.

The most interesting part of this story is that just six weeks later, another runner broke the four-minute barrier.[45] And then in the years that followed, count-less other runners did the same, over and over, until it became routine – until even a few kids in high school managed the feat. What happened? What changed? *Belief.* Other runners broke the same barrier because it was now easier to believe! They knew it could be done. And once this belief set in, of knowing it could be done, the goal became more achievable.

Stories about barriers and limits make me think of fleas in a jar. The only way to keep them from jumping out is by putting a lid on top – a physical barrier. What happens next is fascinating. The fleas keep hitting the lid like popcorn, but with time, the popping slows, and eventually stops altogether. The fleas adjust the height of

---

45 John Landy, who recorded a world-record time of 3:57.9 at an inter-national meet in Finland on 21 June 1954

their jump to avoid hitting the ceiling. At this point, you can remove the lid and the fleas won't jump out. They are trapped by their belief they'll hit the ceiling. They won't jump higher than where the lid used to be − *they won't jump higher than their "belief barrier."*

The analogy to our lives requires no explanation. Our reality − and its inherent limits, barriers, boundaries − is almost entirely defined by what we believe. When the world was flat, distant travel by sea was taboo. But once this archaic belief was broken, seafarers rushed across the Atlantic in mad numbers. *Their belief had changed, and with it, their reality.*

Why People Fail

Studies have demonstrated that people with low self-belief have an expectation of failure, financial difficulty, poor health, troubled relationships, and this usually comes true for them.[46] This mindset creates a self-fulfilling, self-perpetuating prophecy. Because they don't believe they can succeed, they view goals to be tougher than they really are and tend to give up more easily.[47] And when they give up, their failure reinforces their low

---

46 Waitley, D., *Psychology of Success*, McGraw-Hill, 2010

47 Pajares, F., and Schunk, D., Self and Self-Belief in Psychology and Education, in Aronson, J. (Ed.), *Improving Education Achievement*, Academic Press, 2002

self-belief, which makes them give up even more easily in the future. This further validates their mindset that success is impossible. *See, I told you, that kind of success never happens to me,* they remind themselves. At some point, the cycle repeats itself so many times that it becomes truth, gospel.

It's like a boxer walking into the ring thinking, *Look at the shoulders on that guy! There's no way I can win tonight.* And of course, he doesn't win. No surprises there. What the boxer believed would happen, happened. And at the next match, the boxer is more likely to lose, because his low self-belief was reinforced by the prior loss. If you're defeated in the mind, then you're already defeated in reality – you just don't know it yet.

But what causes this mindset? Why do some people look at the success of others and think, *You know, that could never happen to me – I could never achieve that kind of success.* I struggled with this question for years. I wondered if low self-belief was perhaps a guise for laziness, allowing people to justify their lack of desire with the belief "it can't be done." I thought back to my bodybuilding days; it would have been so easy to read Arnold's book and think, *I can never look like that,* and not even try. *Imagine all the hard work I could have saved myself!*

Despite some compelling examples, laziness wasn't the answer. I saw people work tirelessly, two jobs, three, weekends, nights, through sickness and strife, to provide for kids, family, loved ones. *Work!* – like the coalminers, work in endless measure. They weren't lazy. They didn't shrink from the daily grind. And yet, they didn't believe in themselves either – they didn't believe they could achieve success or something better for themselves.

I eventually concluded that self-belief flows from something far more tangible, physical: *our environment.* Psychologists have long held the view that our beliefs, attitudes, and values are largely the product of environmental forces.[48] Consider religion. Your faith is largely determined by where you were born. *Matters of your soul, afterlife, and eternity are determined by geography.* If you were born in Poland, you'd probably become a Roman Catholic. Why? Because 86% of the population is Roman Catholic, because your parents would be Roman Catholic, because your friends would be Roman Catholic, and because you'd experience significant social pressure to become a Roman Catholic. You'd be unlikely to become a Hindu for the simple reason there isn't much Hinduism in Poland. But if you were born in India, the opposite would be true. You'd probably become a Hindu rather than Roman Catholic. Why? Because 82% of the population practises Hinduism, because your parents would be Hindu, because your friends would be Hindu, and because you'd experience significant social pressure to become a Hindu.

---

48 DeAngelis, T., *Are Beliefs Inherited?* American Psychological Association, April 2004

You probably don't realize it, or give it much thought, but your environment has influenced you since the day you were born. From the country, city, and suburb where you grew up, to the friends you kept at school, the environment was always there, in the background, molding you with invisible hands. Even trivial matters – like your accent, vocabulary, and social manners – are all products of your environment. Whether you spit and swear or practise impeccable social etiquette, your behavior is but a manifestation of your environment, of the influences you were exposed to while growing up.

But more important than accents, vocabulary, and behavioral quirks is the influence of our environment on self-belief. The greatest influence from our childhood is what our parents make us believe about ourselves. Some kids are lucky, like me. My parents always said I could do anything, be anyone, and I grew up believing that. The only thing that separated me from what I wanted in life was hard work. I believed that as a child and I believe it now – it's the truth.

Other kids aren't so fortunate. Their parents might neglect them, ignore them, never be around, or tell them they'll never amount to much, that they're nothing special, that there are limits to what they can do in life, to who they can be. Such kids have difficulty in school not because they're incapable of performing well, but because they're incapable of *believing* they can perform well.[49] Studies show that a child's self-belief has more bearing on academic success or failure than actual competence. And when these kids become adults, they spend decades trying to unlearn false beliefs, discovering that the world isn't flat after all, that what others have done, they can also do. Some succeed, others don't. That's why the greatest gift parents can give their children is self-belief. The beliefs kids develop and hold true about themselves become vital forces in their success or failure in everything they do in life.

Divide by Five

The influence of your environment doesn't stop at childhood or even adolescence. It continues into adulthood, mid life, old age, right to the very end. You must become conscious of your environment and the influence it exerts on your life. The implications are enormous, impossible to overstate.

Jim Rohn[50] famously said, "You are the average of the five people you spend the most time with." I believe this is one of the most profound observations in the field

---

49 Pajares, F., and Schunk, D., "Self and Self-Belief in Psychology and Education," in Aronson, J. (Ed.), *Improving Education Achievement*, Academic Press, 2002

50 Emanuel James "Jim" Rohn (1930–2009) was an American entrepreneur, author and motivational speaker, and early mentor of Tony Robbins

of success psychology. The people closest to you have the greatest influence on your life. They influence your values, beliefs, behaviors, decisions, and ultimately, your success or failure. Most likely, you're not even conscious of their influence.

But it's time to wake up.

To fully appreciate Jim's observation and its impact on your financial situation, take a piece of paper and list the five people you spend the most time with. Then, next to each name, *estimate that person's annual income.* In other words, take an educated guess at how much money those closest to you make. Add these numbers together, divide by five, and the result will closely approximate *your* annual income. Like a bullhorn, blast of ice water, broken glass under your feet, this exercise should jolt you. *You are the average of the five people you spend the most time with.* If you spend time with five people who are poor, you'll become the sixth.

And it makes perfect sense.

If the five people closest to you earn an average of $50,000 a year, then you'll be exposed to their beliefs and viewpoints, their friends and peers, their opportunities, and as a result, you'll probably earn what they earn. You'll become a product of *their* environment. But if you spend time with people earning $1 million a year, then you'll be exposed to a different set of beliefs and viewpoints, a different set of friends and peers, different opportunities, and chances are, you'll earn a lot more.

For people earning $50,000 a year, the thought of earning $1 million is abstract, unreal, impossible. If you spend enough time with them, you'll believe the same. *If they can't do it, neither can you.* But for people earning $1 million, it's not abstract, unreal, or impossible. They are walking proof it can be done, right there in front of you. They obviously believe it's possible to earn $1 million a year because they're already doing it. And by spending time with them, you'll also believe it's possible. Like the four-minute mile, you'll see that it's achievable, already done, and your self-belief will climb. What they did, you can do.

I witnessed this effect first-hand when I ran a mentoring program for technology entrepreneurs in Australia. The program consisted of sixteen entrepreneurs who met each month for group mentoring sessions and presentations from successful people. The program ran for two years and the group was exposed to a stream of highly accomplished people each month. The people who came and spoke to the group had sold their businesses for tens of millions of dollars and, in a few cases, like Jud, *hundreds of millions of dollars*. Month in, month out, they came in and matter-of-factly explained how they did it, and I was amazed at the effect these presentations had on the group.

As time passed, the entrepreneurs began to believe that what those successful people had done, they could also do. They had never met people like that before. Up until then, they spent most of their time with other starving entrepreneurs, so no wonder they were starving themselves. Years later, when I caught up with a few of the participants from the program, they told me that those presentations had opened their eyes, shown them what's possible, and changed their belief about what they could achieve.

I had a similar feeling that night I met up with Jud Bowman – his success leapt across the table and smote me like a blow. He cracked ajar bigger doors, doors I had only read about in books. His words were laced with stardust. Spending time with people like Jud forces your self-belief to climb – it has no choice but to climb – a phenomenon that's well documented in psychology studies.[51] Seeing other people succeed raises your self-belief that you can do the same[52] – *if they can do it, so can you!*

Who you spend time with

When I got serious about bodybuilding, I changed gyms to train where the best bodybuilders in town trained. In hindsight, it was the single most important decision

---

51 Bandura, A., *Social Foundations of Thought and Action: A Social-Cognitive Theory*, Prentice Hall, 1986

52 Schunk, D. H., "Modeling and Attributional Feedback Effects on Children's Achievement: A Self-Efficacy Analysis," *Journal of Educational Psychology*, 1981

I made to achieve my bodybuilding goals. All of a sudden, the pictures on my bathroom mirror came to life; I stepped into their world. Many of the bodybuilders had competed in shows and won at various levels. Some were even close to turning pro. Being around them every day at the same gym, doing curls and squats and rows by their side, I knew it was possible. I saw my goals walk and talk in front of me. *I could get there.* Over time, I made friends and received invaluable support. When I hit a plateau, they showed how to break it. When I couldn't get that last bit of fat off my waist, they showed me how to burn it. They encouraged me. Pushed me. Told me I'd succeed if I kept going. They believed and made me believe. It was electric.

But what if I had joined some other gym? Perhaps a general-purpose gym, bereft of bodybuilders, where people thought that bodybuilding was grotesque, unnatural. And each time I came there, they would discourage me, saying my pursuit was foolish, that nothing would ever come of it – what then? What would have happened? I would have failed, that's what. My belief would have faltered. I would have quit, surrendered. I would have become a product of *their* environment.

It doesn't take much imagination to make the leap from bodybuilding to everyday life. In whatever you want to achieve – whether it's financial success, weight loss, a promotion at work, you name it – the people around you will either help or hinder you. If you're trying to lose weight but your friends gorge on fast food, then dieting will be tough. If you want to stay on the right side of the law but your closest friends wear gang colors, then you'll struggle. You'll become a product of their environment, whether you like it or not. So if you spend time with people who complain, whine, steal, abuse, where will you end up? What kind of product will you become?

If you want to achieve your goals, surround yourself with people who have similar goals, or better yet, who *have already achieved them.* If you want to become a straight A student, hang out with straight A students. If you want to become a bodybuilder, spend time with professional bodybuilders. If you want to become a millionaire, spend time with millionaires. These people will directly influence your self-belief. *They've achieved what you want to achieve.* They'll show you how to do it; they'll convince you it's possible. The concrete, no-nonsense way to change your self-belief is to change the factors that influence you.

The key to the Door of Belief is to *change your environment.*

Without mind tricks, without going back in time to relive your childhood, without visiting the shrink for years on end, you can directly and decisively change your self-belief by changing your environment. *Do you want to believe? Do you want to succeed?* Then spend time with people who will help you believe, encourage you to succeed. A positive environment will feed your self-belief like oxygen feeds a flame.

This is the secret behind organizations such as *Weight Watchers* and *Alcoholic Anonymous*. By joining a community of people who share the exact same goal – lose fat and keep it off, or get sober and stay sober – your self-belief will rise. You'll be in a positive environment, surrounded by people who are achieving what you want to achieve. It's as simple as that.

What you put in your mind

But the power of influence goes way beyond people and who you spend time with. In fact, the entire field of marketing is based on influence and persuasion, aimed at building desire for products strong enough to melt credit cards. So whether you realize it or not, you're being influenced *all the time*. Everything you read, see, and hear influences you. *I'm influencing you right now.* You may do something different today, tomorrow, next week because of what I say. Wake up! Snap out of it! Become conscious of your environment, *become conscious of what you put into your head.* You are in control. You don't have to sit in front of the television and fritter your life away on games or senseless shows. Go to the library, borrow books, subscribe to blogs, download podcasts, discover the world, get inspired.

What you put in your mind has the same effect as the people you spend time with. Positive material can send your self-belief soaring – all you have to do is spend some time online, at the library; there's a world of information at your fingertips. Read about Michael Dell, how he started Dell Computer with $1000 at the age of nineteen and became a billionaire in the process. Discover Frank Lowy, the penniless immigrant who learned English, business, and built Westfield Group from nothing into the multi-billion-dollar empire it is today. Be amazed by Arnold Schwarzenegger, how he conquered body-building, then business, then Hollywood, and finally politics. Do you think you can learn from these people? Do you think their stories will influence you? build your self-belief? feed your mind with positive thoughts and messages? Of course they will. The immeasurable wealth of human knowledge and triumph is waiting for you, sitting idly on hard drives and library shelves around the world.

In my younger days, when I was cramming my mind with endless books, I didn't understand how they were influencing me. But they were. Instead of hanging out with friends who wanted to booze up on the weekend, I was being influenced by books on success, achievement, and ceilings that could never be reached. And even though I didn't know it at the time, the books were stoking my self-belief to untold heights. The more I read, the more I believed in myself. And that self-belief then spilled over from bodybuilding into every nook and cranny of my life – success seemed inevitable in anything I wanted to tackle.

The kid in the ghetto

But my situation is different, I can hear a million readers whimper. The gym begins to fade from view. The groans and moans, the sticky atmosphere, humid with sweat, tears, and agony, grows dim and distant. In its place, I see a kid in the slums. He's living in a broken home, a dump, the very worst of environments. His brother is in prison, his father, dead. His room is bare, unclean, lit by a single, weak bulb humming erratically overhead. He's surrounded by pessimism, hopelessness; everything that's dirty and vulgar in life is pulling him down, deeper, further, until surrender seems inevitable.

And yet, something inside him resists the downward march. The tiniest flicker of desire, too small to measure, goads him to buy *Life in Half a Second.* I see him lying in bed, reading this book, this very chapter on belief, and I watch his lips. They move sluggishly, deliberately, into a sneer. He stops reading and looks up at me. Across the vastness that separates us, our eyes meet.

"Yeah, I wanna to be rich – who don't?" he confesses. *"But look at me.* Look where I'm at. What can I do? No rich folk will hang with me!"

His stare is a taunt, his words a challenge that cannot be answered. He believes that his situation is hopeless, beyond redemption. *But he's wrong.* Absolutely wrong. And as I watch this kid, reading my book and sneering, I steel myself to his challenge; I answer his question.

"What can you do? Everything. Surround yourself by the rich folks in books, magazines, online. Go to the library and read all you can," I preach to him. "Discover a role model. Spend time with your teachers, meet their friends. Find a mentor. Save a few dollars. Then pack your stuff and get the hell out of there, go upstate, into the suburbs. Get a job, finish school, live on the cheap in a student apartment. And keep filling your head with can-do material and information."

And as my fingers dance across the keys, speaking to the kid in the ghetto, I can feel nodules of sweat break through my skin, gaining size, weight; I am in a fever now, burning, pitched high with anticipation. *What will he do?* I wait and I watch. And then, movement, spontaneous combustion, the flicker of desire bursts into flame. I see this kid rise from his bed, his house, his environment, and escape from the clutches of self-destruction. His shoulders straighten as he changes friends, where he lives, what he puts into his head. I hardly recognize him. He's in control now, total control. He's conscious of his environment and its influence. He believes in himself, he knows he can go places, do things. The power is all his. He looks back over his shoulder, his sneer now a smile, and then never looks back again.

Now, I've never lived in the ghetto, I don't know what it's like, and my impression of it might be naïve, sophomoric. But what I do know, beyond doubt or dispute, is that *anyone* can change their environment if they want to, if their desire is strong enough, and when they change their environment, their self-belief will change with it. Studies have proven this time and time again.[53] And so we return to desire, because it's the only thing that will get this kid out of the ghetto, out of his environment.

Anyone living in the ghetto can pack their bags and move. We all have choice, freewill. But the decision is driven by desire. If you hate the ghetto – whatever your particular "ghetto" may be – but don't move, it means your desire hasn't reached the tipping point, the same tipping point needed to start a diet, end an abusive relationship, go back to school, quit drugs, start a business, and every other challenging endeavor.

Are you fully awake yet? completely conscious? Take a look at your goals and then your environment. With a critical eye, assess what you read, watch, and who you associate with. Everything exerts influence – books, television, friends, family, school, *everything*. Is your environment helping you or hindering you? Are you surrounding

---

53 Bandura, A., *Social Foundations of Thought and Action: A Social-Cognitive Theory*, Prentice Hall, 1986

yourself with successful people – people who have achieved what you want to achieve? Are you reading their biographies? Subscribing to their blogs? Going to events where they speak and lecture? Are you living in the right place? Receiving the right kind of education? Filling your RSS feeds with useful information? If not, *what are you going to do about it?*

Nothing?

Then I question your desire. You're not serious. You're pretending, fooling yourself. Go back to the second door and align your goals with your desire. Now that you're conscious of your environment and its influence, you must change whatever needs changing. You can't do anything about the past, your childhood is what it is, but the future is unwritten, up to you. *It's your life, your half second.* All the decisions, all the choices, are yours. You're in control.

Action Items

Research has conclusively demonstrated that people with low self-belief have low aspirations and weak commitment to the goals they set. They slacken their efforts and give up quickly in the face of difficulties.[54] Remember *The Empire Strikes Back*? The scene where Luke Skywalker tries to get his fighter plane out of the swamp but fails in the attempt? Yoda then steps up, closes his eyes, and with outstretched arms, pulls the plane from the mud and onto dry land.

Luke stares in wonder. "I don't believe it!" he says.

Yoda looks at him, sighs, and replies, "That is why you fail."

It's a poignant moment, a reminder that success requires self-belief. It's not optional. You *must* believe in yourself; you must believe you can achieve your goals. Without belief, you'll become your own worst enemy. Your mind will force your heart to surrender.

To walk through the third door of success:

- *Evaluate your environment.* List the people you spend the most time with, the television shows you watch, the sites you visit on the internet, the books you read – *analyze how you spend your time.* Think of yourself as an accountant, auditing the precious minutes and hours you spend each day. Now compare this list of influences with your goals and identify what helps, what hinders, and what makes no difference.

---

54 Bandura, A., "Perceived Self-Efficacy in Cognitive Development and Functioning," *Educational Psychologist*, April 1993

- *Change your environment.* Start with the things that hinder you the most and tackle these immediately. If they seem "too hard," then revisit your desire: *you don't want it bad enough.* Like the kid in the ghetto, bold change is fuelled by bold desire. The easiest change will be what goes inside your head – books, websites, blogs, television. Changing social circles will be harder. And hardest of all will be uprooting yourself (if necessary). But no matter how daunting the change, remember that you're in control – you can design your life by choosing *who* and *what* you surround yourself with. It's up to you.

- *Keep track of your progress.* Buy a pocket-sized diary and write down three things each day that contributed to your goals. It might have been something that happened at work, at school, a new relationship you've developed, a book you're reading – write it down. This exercise taps into Reticular Activation, discussed in the Door of Clarity. It will train your mind to "see" the progress you're making towards your goals, which in turn will increase your self-belief.[55] The more progress you see, the more achievable your goals will seem. It will only cost you three minutes each day, so get the diary and do

---

55 People suffering from depression can improve their mental well-being by writing down three happy moments that occurred each day. By using Reticular Activation, they train their mind to focus on the positive aspects of life. Studies have shown that in as little as fourteen days, their mental state significantly improves because they begin to see more positives than negatives. Just like the simple exercise in the Door of Clarity of looking for red items, then closing your eyes and trying to recall green items. Reticular Activation works.

this exercise, *every day.* Even if what you write are trivial items, do it. No excuses.

By knowing exactly what you want, wanting it badly, and believing you can get it, you have primed your mind for success. You have given yourself the absolute best possible chance of achieving your goals. Clarity, desire, and belief are working together on your behalf, night and day in your subconscious. You have presented your mind with a tangible, concrete problem: *How can I get what I want? How can I achieve my goals?* Your mind is not drifting, wandering; it's working on this problem non-stop, trying to solve it, trying to make it happen. Every meeting you have, every human interaction, every piece of information you put inside your head is now viewed against the contextual backdrop of your goals. *You're on your way!*

"I only want to do what others have done before me."
Jack London

The Fourth Door

A thousand kilometers west of Ecuador, jutting from the depths of the Pacific Ocean like skyscrapers piercing the smog of modern life, lies an oasis of sorts, immortalized by Charles Darwin and *The Voyage of the Beagle*. Some 170 years after the great man's visit to the Galapagos Islands, I traced his footsteps across the wild, untamed terrain, wading through flocks of birds and colonies of reptiles, seeing them co-exist, fearless of humans, and free from the vexations of predators.

I had imagined the islands to be serene, pristine, a place where philosophical thought is hatched and enlightenment found. *Boy was I naïve!* From the moment my foot touched land, I was under siege. Birds screeched overhead, fighting aerial battles, using beaks as sabres and wings as shields. The iguanas were duelling, headbutting each other with the force of gunshots cracking through the air. And on the jagged rocks, defending the coastline, were the sumo-wrestling sea lions, jostling and body slapping, their struggles reverberating through the hills with deep, dull thuds. The wildlife that wasn't fighting, watched, and participated in other ways: the frigatebirds inflated their flame-red throat sacs, iguanas changed color, and the albatrosses practised their courtship dance. And blanketing the landscape in every possible direction was dung and crap and fecal matter, absolutely everywhere, courtesy of the brimming wildlife that ate, slept, and did their business all in the same spot. It was a luxury just to stand on clean dirt.

"This is madness," I told the guide.

"This is life," he corrected me. "This is the animal kingdom."

Animals? Life? The scene reminded me of high school, especially the student assemblies every few months. The teachers would herd us into the main hall, where the antics would begin and continue for the better part of an hour. Knowing that all the females were there, watching, pointing, whispering, and giggling, the males would show off, each attempting to outdo the other. Their gaudy clothes, gadgets, earrings, piercings – all of it – were attempts to stand out, woo, and seduce, no different to the red throat sac of frigatebirds or the mating colors of marine iguanas. And the result was the same: *madness.*

The last assembly I attended began like any other. I remember sitting in the audience, trying to anticipate the flying projectiles that were being hurled about. A broken marble and chewed-up piece of gum were in the mix, searching for a square forehead or soft patch of hair. I pulled my baseball cap down, wondering why I hadn't feigned sickness that day. *I hated assemblies.* But I was glad I came, as the event took an unexpected turn.

The school had invited a guest speaker who entered the stage alongside the principal. He was dressed like money: a dark blue suit, yellow tie, and shoes that glossed from a mile away. The principal's introduction was greeted by an embarrassing cacophony of hee-hawing, body slapping, and screeching. The herd didn't pay attention. They didn't have time. They were too busy puffing their chests and preening.

The speaker then reached the podium, put his hands on either side, and began to speak. And as he did so, the jostling, headbutting, and body slapping immediately died. The man had said something crazy, insane, and the herd had missed it. They looked at him in anticipation, wanting to hear it again.

The man waited for the silence to take effect. "That's right, you heard me," he said. "If you're *not* going to college, then quit school *today!*"

Disbelief pulsed and surged through the hall, peaking in a crescendo of grunts, snorts, and hysterical bleating.

The kid next to me tugged wildly on my arm. "Did he just say we should drop out of school?" he panted. "Who is this guy? I like him!"

There was absolute silence now; the attention was all his. I could hear myself breathe as he scanned the assembly hall, left to right, top to bottom.

"Quit school today," he continued, "*because McDonald's needs you.*"

The hee-hawing and body slapping exploded again. The mammals edged forward, jostling one another to get a closer look, a better listen. *This man was mad!* But mad or not, he had their attention.

"You're all so cool, with your faded jeans, Mustangs, tailgate parties – man, *I wish I could be as cool as you!*" he thundered, his voice splitting the air like a bullwhip. "But you know what, on second thought, living with your parents, driving your mama's car, sponging off your family for clothes, food, and dates, and drinking booze in back alleys – you know, that ain't so cool after all."

His words fell like sledgehammers, smashing through thin veneers, exposing truth, and leaving behind a cruel vacuum that no one dared to fill.

"Do you want to know what *cool* is?"

The crowd craned its neck. *They wanted to know.*

"Cool is having your own house, driving your own car. Cool is being able to travel the world, party in London, Madrid. Cool is drinking champagne on the Eiffel Tower at a quarter to midnight. That's what *cool* is. Not the hill-billy stuff you do. That's for kids. Toddlers."

The man paused, smiling ever so slightly.

"If you want to be cool in the real world – the *adult* world – do something with your life, become somebody, *and use your mind to do it.* Then you'll be cool." Another pause, another smile. "But that's never gonna happen unless you *invest in yourself* – in your education, in your future. Without college, you'll always be driving your mama's car. Without college, what's the point of a high school diploma? You'll earn the same with or without it – *minimum wage.* So if you're not going to college, quit school *today.* McDonald's needs you, they're short on staff, they have openings – *go there now.*"

I had already enrolled at the university for one class per semester, so I breathed easy. But not everyone was breathing easy. Into the menagerie had come a man. He had cracked his whip and made the quivering mass of wildlife assess their place in the food chain. And the wildlife realized, with dwindling self-regard, that their place was low. The more the man spoke – about education, college, using your brain and becoming somebody in the world – the more they realized they were no better than worms wriggling on the ground. He showed them truth that was dark, terrifying – truth as bleak and pulseless as the emptiness of space. And having frightened them with darkness and fire, he then showed them how to rise up, above the dirt and dung, above the screeching and thumping and body slapping, and stand, on two feet, and think, reason, reaching upwards, towards the light, to become somebody. It was through education, through putting something into your head, making your mind valuable. *That was the secret.*

Some kids woke up that day, became conscious, and realized they were still children. What they regarded as cool was only cool in a child's world, and soon, very soon, they would become adults, and as adults, they wouldn't be cool anymore. Without college, education, career, they would be no better than the unthinking creatures on the ground, squabbling among filth, ignorance, and irrelevance. *Get an education,* is what the man had said. *Go to college. Use your mind.*

What You Know

Big goals are never easy goals. You can define them with absolute clarity. You can commit them to paper, review them, tell friends and family, visualize them, search your heart and align them to your deepest desires. You can change your environment, change your belief. And despite it all, *nothing.* Year in, year out, your big goals elude you. What you *really* want in life – what you long for, dream about, pine over – remains stubbornly out of reach. Is there some invisible force working against you? An undercurrent preventing you from reaching success?

There is – and it's called *ignorance.*

You will never achieve your big goals if you don't know *how* to achieve them. You can have absolute clarity about the future, about where you want to go, but if you don't know *how* to get there, if the path is unknown, undiscovered, you'll get lost along the way. Everything in life is easier if you know how to do it. Don't believe me? Then try assembling a car engine without a guide or instructions. See how that goes. Studies have shown it's easier to achieve success if you know *how* to achieve it.[56]

Imagine that your financial situation tops your list of negatives. You're determined to change it. And not in some incremental manner, but in a major, *life-changing* way. You're tired of juggling credit cards, overdue bills, living from paycheck to paycheck. You want to be successful, *financially* successful. Over the years, you've met a few people who drove Ferraris. They always seemed cool and collected. They didn't worry about grocery bills or paying rent each month. They didn't struggle. And that's what you want: *to end the struggle.* So you frame your big goal as something tangible, concrete, audacious: *a Ferrari.* The car represents financial success – if you can afford a Ferrari, then you won't be worrying about grocery bills or rent. You will have made it. The car provides your mind with a vivid picture of "financial success" – of

---

56 Hawley, K., "Success and Knowledge," *American Philosophical Quarterly,* University of Illinois Press, 2003

what "having enough" looks like. *You want to have enough.* The goal seems impossible, but you've been reading *Life in Half a Second*, door by door, and you decide to go for it. You want to buy a Ferrari within three years of today – it's your three-year goal. *You see it, want it, and believe it.*

A picture of the Ferrari appears on your bathroom mirror, your desk at work, your refrigerator. At night you can see the car under your eyelids – you open the door, fall into the bucket seat, push the start button. You're flying through hills, tunnels, slicing through air, engine screaming, climaxing, the sounds and colors running together, blurring, like paint on water, just as sleep overtakes your senses. During the day you stare at the pictures, at night you animate them in your mind.

But weeks pass, months, and still no Ferrari. You surround yourself with more pictures. You visit the Ferrari dealership to touch the car, sit in it. You attend Ferrari club meetings as a guest, speak to owners, admire their cars. More weeks and months pass. They turn into years. And no matter how many times you picture the prancing horse in your garage, no matter how many times you chant, *I want a Ferrari! I want a Ferrari! I want a Ferrari!* the car doesn't materialize. Time is ticking and you're somehow unable to force a ton of rubber, plastic, and metal to twist itself into parts and paint, and spontaneously assemble in your driveway. Every morning you check, anxiously peering through the window, hoping, but nothing. You're still juggling credit cards, overdue bills, living from paycheck to paycheck, and each morning the driveway remains empty.

I love visualization, absolutely love it. But I know that visualization by itself won't make the Ferrari materialize. Between *visualizing* the car and *possessing* the car, much has to happen. You have to become financially successful in order to buy the car. But *how*? What *exactly* should you do? And right there lies the problem – you don't know. Clarity, desire, belief – they're all there – and yet, no Ferrari. Something is wrong. If this book ended on the last door, you'd send it back for a refund, donate it to the library, shred it, burn it in the gutter. *Clarity, desire, and belief aren't enough.* Something is missing. But what?

In one word: *Knowledge* – the fourth door of success.

Between your current state of struggling and worrying about money, and your goal of being financially successful and owning a Ferrari, there are many steps in between – an entire path. The problem is, you're clueless about what that path looks like, and you can't get to your goal without it. You're lost, adrift, not knowing what to do next, or how to do it. You have everything in place, except knowledge. You're clear about what you want, you want it badly, believe yourself capable of getting it, but you don't know *how* to get it. The fourth door of success is about the "how."

Different paths to success

To reach any goal, there are many paths you can follow. Some paths are short but risky, while others are safe but long. You could travel across a mountain range on a narrow path characterized by vertical drops and avalanches, or you could circumvent the mountains on a wide, flat path. The one through the mountains is dangerous, but takes ten days, whereas the other is safe and sure, but takes a year.

If you define "financial success" as one million dollars – a nice round number that would swiftly end your financial worries and secure a Ferrari – many paths can take you there. The wide, safe path, advocated by financial planners and retirement books around the world, is to save and invest money each month. If you save $287 per month and invest at 8% annually, you will have $1,000,000 in 40 years. You can reduce the time by saving more or finding better investments, but in either case, the road is still a long one – many decades. A faster path would be through real estate, buying homes, renovating them, and then reselling. An even faster path would be through starting your own business or buying a franchise. *The time is getting shorter, but the path is also getting higher and narrower.* The fastest path would be through speculation – in stocks, currencies, commodities – or outright gambling in casinos and racetracks. These paths are very short, as people have won millions of dollars in Reno and Vegas, but they're also exceedingly high and narrow, as evidenced by the countless gamblers who have slipped from dizzying heights never to rise again.

The Door of Knowledge isn't about *which* path you take; it's about *knowing* the paths and their characteristics – *narrow and tall, but fast, or wide and flat, but long.* Getting to bodybuilding success, a Ferrari, million dollars – to *any* goal – is a hundred times easier if you know the path. And the more paths you know, the more choices and options you'll have. You can balance risk, time, and other factors by choosing the path that best fits your life situation and personality. But if you don't know the path, then you're just stumbling in the dark, feeling along the walls, no different to the boy searching for water in the cave. And you remember what happened to him, right?

Without knowing the paths that lead to your goal, you are severely handicapped. Think about something as straightforward as dieting. Say you have a precise goal of losing twenty pounds of fat within six months. You're overweight, and your desire to lose weight has reached the tipping point. You have friends who have shed their jelly-rolls, and if they can do it, so can you. *So far so good.* But here comes the problem: *what exactly should you do?* What are the paths to fat loss? What are trade-offs between time, safety, and sustainability? Should you cut your calories in half? Go on the low-carb diet? Low-fat diet?

And what about exercise? Should you use free weights? machines? aerobics? a combination? Perhaps interval training followed by steady-state aerobics? The questions are endless, and without knowing the answers, you're back in the cave, groping your way through darkness.

Knowledge and self-belief

Aside from being a fundamental factor in achieving success, knowledge also plays a large role in developing self-belief. If you interview one hundred entrepreneurs who are starting their first business, and ask them if they believe they can build a $100 million company, the vast majority will say "no." Why? Because they don't know *how* to build a $100 million business – they've never done it before. They lack the knowledge and experience. They're worried about making their business viable, rather than building an empire. But if you pose the same question to a hundred entrepreneurs who *have* built a $100 million company, the answer will be different. The vast majority will say "yes." One group believes they can do it, the other doesn't.

What's the difference? *Knowledge.*

One group knows how to build a $100 million company, the other doesn't. And their knowledge directly impacts their belief. If those first-time entrepreneurs want to build a $100 million company, they'll need to acquire the knowledge – either through direct education, hiring experienced people, or both. Without knowledge, failure is the likely result.[57]

Given the close relationship between knowledge and belief, it's no surprise they come from the same place: *your environment.* If your parents were successful entrepreneurs, you'd have the knowledge and self-belief to become an entrepreneur by the time you reached high school. If your parents were lawyers, nothing would be simpler and more straightforward than becoming a lawyer. *Politics? Show business?* The same. That's why so many kids follow in their parents' footsteps. The path their parents took to achieve success is visible to them. The mystery of becoming a millionaire, politician, actor, musician, lawyer, or doctor is explained, in plain English, over the dinner table. The fourth door of success is cracked open at an early age.

The importance of your environment cannot be overstated. By spending time with successful people – whether in business, politics, sports, or some other field – you'll learn what path they took, what the risks were, how long it took. And by raising your knowledge, you'll raise your self-belief. It's like the mentoring program I ran for technology entrepreneurs in Australia. Each month, the entrepreneurs met someone who had sold their business for tens of millions of dollars, and each month they heard

---

57 Lack of knowledge and experience is the primary reason why the majority of new businesses fail within a few years of starting up. First-time entrepreneurs don't know what they don't know.

the same story, over and over, until the path became clear. And as their knowledge grew, their self-belief grew with it. *What those successful people had done, they could also do.*

The Goal Pyramid

Without knowledge, your goals will remain elusive, out of reach, like the Ferrari in the driveway. *That's the bad news.* The good news is that all the knowledge you need to succeed already exists. It's all out there, waiting for you. You won't be the first person to lose twenty pounds, buy a Ferrari, or build a $100 million company – it's all been done before, all of it. Even if you want to break a sports record or make a medical discovery, plenty of people have broken records and made discoveries before you. *How did they do it?* You can follow their example by discovering the path they took.

When Arnold Schwarzenegger hatched his dream of becoming a world-champion bodybuilder and then parlaying his success into movies, he wasn't the first person to do so. He was following in the footsteps of giants before him, giants like Reg Park and Steve Reeves, who themselves were following in the footsteps of other giants before them who had successfully transitioned from sports into show business.

You don't have to beat a new path across the jungle to reach success. Whatever your goals are, just discover the path taken by those before you. Once you know the path, you won't need to rely on wishful thinking. You'll know what to do. You'll stop chanting *I want a Ferrari!* and start moving down the path that leads to the car.

The knowledge will empower you.

But just because you know the path, doesn't mean you'll get there overnight. Few people are dead broke one day only to wake up as millionaires the next. It doesn't work that way. It took Arnold Schwarzenegger almost a decade to conquer the sport of bodybuilding, and another decade to make a successful transition into show business. The achievement of big goals – whether it's a Ferrari, million dollars, or movie stardom – is based on the achievement of many milestones that ultimately culminate in success:

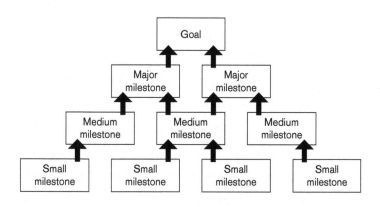

I've used this "goal pyramid" for decades – in body-building, business, book writing – in anything and everything I've undertaken. I've also applied it to the lives of hundreds of entrepreneurs that have come through my workshops and mentoring programs. The goal pyramid is a knowledge tool, which maps the path to success by breaking down goals into milestones. By achieving the milestones, you'll achieve the goal at the top. If your pyramid has blanks in it, it means you still don't know the entire path. But like a jigsaw puzzle, you now have some of the pieces and it's easier to fill in the rest. Research shows that unpacking a goal into milestones can make the goal more manageable and increase your effort and performance to achieve it.[58]

If you want to become a film director, directing big-budget feature films, then your goal pyramid might look like this:

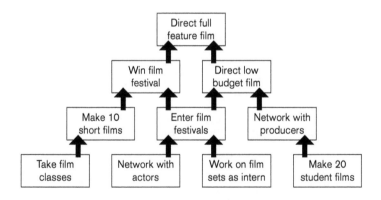

You can think of the bottom milestones as one-year goals, the middle two layers as three-year goals, and the

---

58 Grohol, J., "Visualize Your Goal in Order to Attain It," *PsychCentral*, 16 August 2011

capstone as the five-year goal. That's a path you can follow. It doesn't guarantee success, but you now know what the path looks like, what the steps are. It's all there in black and white, demystified – no wishful thinking required. Many of the world's best-known directors followed a similar path, such as Martin Scorsese, an NYU film student who made a series of well-received short films before going on to make *Taxi Driver*, *Goodfellas*, *The Aviator*, *Shutter Island*, and countless other blockbusters. Or Quentin Tarantino, who directed and starred in short films before writing and directing the hit *Pulp Fiction*.

From directing films to advancing your career, any promotion in any company can be mapped out using a goal pyramid:

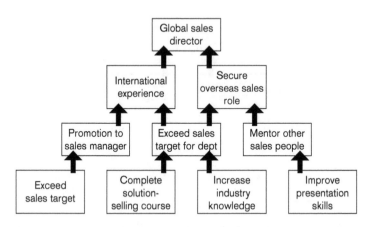

Consider that Jack Welch planned his path to the CEO position at General Electric using a similar approach.[59]

---

59 Bryne, J., "How Jack Welch Runs GE," *Business Week*, 8 June 1998

Or you might be an entrepreneur, starting a new business and needing to raise money from investors. In that case, the goal of raising money would be at the top of the pyramid, supported by the necessary milestones to make it happen:

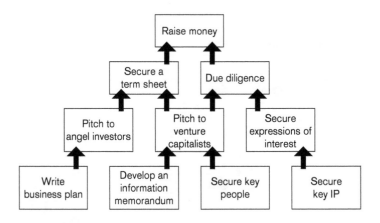

This pyramid is much easier to climb than becoming a film director or securing a global sales role, and reaching the top can be done in less than six months.

When you reach the top, start over

Once you reach the top of your goal pyramid, whatever it may be, an interesting thing happens: *the top of the pyramid becomes the bottom.* In the previous pyramid, of raising money for an entrepreneurial business, the top of the pyramid drops to the bottom once the goal is achieved.

Once you succeed in raising capital, you move to a new goal pyramid – perhaps to build a $10 million company, with milestones for hiring sales people, opening offices,

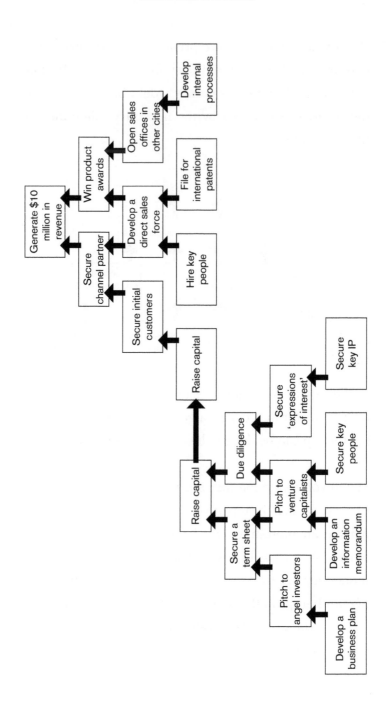

building partnerships, as shown above. And when you achieve that, there will be more goals, more pyramids. That's how a $100 million company is built, how the CEO's chair is attained, how any large goal is achieved: *step by step, milestone by milestone.* When you reach the top of any pyramid, whether in business, movies, sports, or some other domain, a new one should take its place. That's how extraordinary success is achieved: *by climbing to new heights on the backs of goals you've already achieved.*

There should never be a time when there's nothing new for you to move on to. Even if financial independence or retirement is your top goal, once achieved, it should drop to the bottom of your next pyramid, whatever it may be: sailing around the world, touring the Himalayas, writing a book, spending time with loved ones. It doesn't matter what, but there should always be something beyond your current goals. If there's not, what will you do? *Stare into space? Lie on the beach? Die?* After retiring from work, many people suffer depression for exactly this reason.[60] There's nothing new for them to move on to, no new pyramid to tackle.

Connecting goals and milestones to tasks

Using a goal pyramid to define the path to success is no different to how a business operates. The management team sets a strategic five-year goal, typically defined in terms

---

60 "Beating Depression After Retirement," *Health24*, 4 April 2013; and Bercier, S., *Depression in Retirement*, Retirement Planning Institute

of revenue, profit, market share, and other such metrics. This five-year goal is then broken down into annual goals, which are further broken down into quarterly and monthly targets. And on a weekly basis, the management team meets to discuss progress towards the monthly targets. Hence, the five-year goal stretches all the way down to daily activities. By achieving the monthly and quarterly targets, management will achieve the annual goals. And by achieving the annual goals, management will achieve the five-year goal – the top of the pyramid. And that's how bonuses and promotions happen: by achieving business goals.

The lesson here is that your big goals must be connected to your daily activities – you must be working towards your milestones and goals on a *daily basis*. And the way to establish this connection is quite straightforward. First you discover the path to your big goal and convert it into milestones. This process is equivalent to breaking down a five-year business goal into annual, quarterly, and monthly targets. *The five-year business goal cannot be achieved without first achieving the annual goals.* Then you connect your milestones to your daily life through *weekly tasks*.

In the goal pyramid above of becoming a *Global Sales Director*, the bottom-level milestones are to exceed your sales target, complete a solution-selling course, increase your industry knowledge, and improve your presentation skills. To achieve these milestones, your weekly tasks might be to make a specified number of customer calls, meetings, and presentations, sign up for a solution-selling course, attend events organized by industry associations, and work with a coach to improve your sales pitch. Completing these and other tasks each week will ensure progress towards the milestones each week.

The achievement of any big goal requires a thousand little steps, and those weekly tasks are your steps. In the same way that milestones move you closer to goals, weekly tasks move you closer to milestones. You're connecting your big goals – which may be years into the future – with your weekly activities. Most people know that Arnold Schwarzenegger's goal was to become a world-champion bodybuilder. But what most people don't know is that he wrote down his entire workout on a chalkboard each morning at the gym, right down to the exact exercise and number of sets. As he completed each exercise, he would cross it off the chalkboard, until his whole workout was done. His ultimate goal was connected to what he did on a daily basis.

Before I wrote my first business book, *Winning Credibility: A guide for building a business from rags to riches,* I first sought knowledge about becoming a published author. I read books on becoming a writer, attended writing conferences, and met with published authors. Once I discovered the path, I created a goal pyramid. At the top was for *Winning Credibility* to become a financial success for the publisher. Being an author wasn't enough; *I wanted to be a successful author.* To achieve this goal, the largest milestone was to get the book published, and the milestone right below that was to actually write the book. Besides stamping out the 76,000 words that would become *Winning Credibility*, there were plenty of other milestones, such as finding an agent, having the draft critiqued, hiring a publicist, securing a publisher, and more. Each week I created a new list of tasks, such as finishing a chapter or segment, incorporating feedback from reviewers, sending letters to agents and publishers, and meeting with authors. And each week, I got a little closer to my milestones. The goal became connected to my weekly activities in a very tangible way.

And in the years since *Winning Credibility*, nothing has changed. There's a goal pyramid hanging on the wall beside me, a few inches from my computer screen, with the milestones for *Life in Half a Second*. I'm moving up that pyramid, week by week, milestone by milestone, knowing that my weekly tasks are bringing the publication date closer at hand. And the sheer fact that you're reading this sentence means that I've completed my goal pyramid for *Life in Half a Second* and have moved on to something new.

The goal pyramid works. It doesn't rely on gimmicks or mind tricks. And everything I do in life – whether it's writing a book or building a business – I do in the same way: I set goals that are aligned to my desire; I change my environment to increase my knowledge and self-belief; I map out the paths to success and evaluate the trade-offs; I create a goal pyramid and define the milestones; and finally, I get to work on my weekly tasks! From my biggest goal all the way down to the most trivial task, everything is connected. I never feel helpless, peering out the window each morning, checking the driveway. *I know what to do.* And nothing in life is difficult if you know what to do.

Your Greatest Asset

Imagine that you own a factory with a single machine. Every dollar the factory earns comes from that one machine. When running at peak performance, the machine spews money into the air like an oil well, but when it breaks down, the well runs dry. You want to buy another machine, to diversify your risk and income, but can't – the machine is the last of its kind. Nothing can replace it. Once it wears out, that's it: *no more machine, no more income.* You'll have to close the factory when that day comes. Knowing this, you do everything humanly possible to keep the machine running. You invest in the machine religiously, even buying a blanket to keep it warm at night. If the machine stops, your income will stop. That machine is your greatest asset.

Well guess what – *that machine is you.*

You are your greatest asset. Not your business, house, job, or retirement savings, but *you*. You've created all those things in your life, you've made them happen. And so if you're going to invest in anything, invest in yourself, the greatest asset you'll ever have. From all the money you put into stocks, bonds, and real estate during your lifetime, the largest return will always come from the investment you make in yourself. There would be no stocks, bonds, and real estate without *you*. And if you won't take investment advice from me, then take it from the most successful investor of all time, Warren Buffet, who believes that "The best investment you can make is an investment in yourself."[61]

The key to the Door of Knowledge is to *invest in yourself.*

And thinking back to that high school assembly, to the man who cracked his whip and frightened the herd with darkness and fire, that was his message – that was the fundamental truth he wanted to implant into our primitive skulls. *Invest in yourself, in your education, in your future,* is what he had said. It's such an obvious statement; everyone agrees with it. But when it comes to doing it, to actually pushing money across the counter, it suddenly becomes much less obvious. The irony of success and failure is that

61 Venables, M., "Warren Buffet on Teaching Kids Smart Investing," *Forbes*, 27 March 2013

we are reluctant to invest in the one asset that can take us to success. It doesn't make sense. We don't think twice about buying a new television, phone, tablet, gadget – things we'll toss in the recycling bin a few years later – but when it comes to investing in our greatest asset, ourselves, we pause, cuddle our wallet, hesitate. *Knowledge is expensive*, we think, *education costs too much*. And we put our wallet away. Well, if you think knowledge is expensive, try ignorance.

Ignorance is the most expensive thing in the world.

Knowing "what" versus knowing "how"

Knowing the path – knowing *what* to do – is only half the equation. The other half is knowing *how* to do it. You may know that lifting weights will tone your body. You may even know the exact routine to follow. But do you know *how* to lift weights? Do you know how to correctly perform a squat, shoulder press, or seated row? Where to position your feet? How to stabilize your lower back? The full range of motion? How to breathe? When to breathe? Knowing *what* and knowing *how* are two different things.

To become a movie director, you may know that the path lies through making short films and winning acclaim at film festivals. That much is clear. But do you know *how* to make a short film? *Scripts, camera lens, angles, long shots, master shots, lighting, blocking, soundtrack, editing?* Again, knowing *what to do* allows you to see the path; knowing *how to do it* allows you to follow the path.

119

You may know the path to becoming a published author, but do you know how to write? How to create a layered plot, three-dimensional characters, subtext through word choice and sentence structure? You may know the path to raising capital for your business, but do you know how to write a compelling business plan? find investors? pitch your plan? navigate your way through due diligence and term sheets?

Without knowing how to do something, you'll invariably make mistakes. And the cost of those mistakes will far exceed the cost of educating yourself in the first place. I've seen it over and over, countless times, in every possible variation. Retirees who skimped on financial advice, only to reach their golden years broke. Dieters who ended up with injuries or worse, because they avoided the cost of a personal trainer. Or entrepreneurs who saved money on business plan coaching, only to end up with a plan that got them nowhere, wasting months or years of their life in the process.

Ignorance hurts, ignorance is expensive. Without investing in yourself, how are you expecting to achieve your big goals? *Through luck? chance? happenstance?* To achieve big goals, you must discover the different paths, their pros and cons, and the milestones along the way. You must then invest in yourself to acquire the necessary skills and knowledge to achieve the milestones – perhaps through schooling, training, reading, accreditation, mentoring, or something else. Whatever is required, do it, make the investment. That's the real path to success. Not wishful thinking, gimmicks, or tricks. It's the feet-on-the-ground way to achieve your goals, in the same manner others have achieved them before you.

The exchange rate between "life" and "cash"

When I was growing up, nothing was ever given to me. If I wanted something, I had to work for it. And so I entered the workforce at the age of sixteen, earning the minimum wage of $4.25 an hour at Target stores. Each weekend, I showed up for work in my red shirt and khaki pants, ready to exchange 20 hours of my life for $85. I knew that "time is money," but while working at Target, I realized that money was more than just time: *money was life.*

When I bought something for $85, I wasn't just spending $85, I was spending 20 hours of my life – 20 hours of standing behind a cash register, waiting on people, with stiff legs, aching back, bored, uncomfortable, dejected – 20 hours I could never get back. What I bought might have been worth $85, *but was it worth 20 hours of my life?* That was the real question.

I began to understand the value of money, and more than that, I began to understand the value of life. The things I bought were not cheap or expensive based on the amount of dollars they cost – they were cheap or expensive based on the amount of life I gave up to earn those dollars. Target was converting my "life" into cash, no different to a casino converting cash into chips so you don't feel like you're spending real money. *Chips are more abstract than bills and coins.* And by the same token, *bills and coins are more abstract than life.* Once I became conscious of the connection between money and life, I wanted to make things cheaper for myself by improving the exchange rate between "life" and "cash."

With this in mind, I moved from Target to fast food for an extra 50 cents per hour, and kept moving from one chain to another until I maxed out at the lofty rate of $5.50. I was now converting life into cash at the rate of $5.50 per hour, an improvement of more than 20%. I then changed industries into grocery retail for $5.75, and a few months later, moved to a competitor for $6 an hour. But it was hopeless. I felt hopeless. I was so much meat and bone, worth so many dollars and cents per hour, depending on how much I packed, cooked, or lifted.

It wasn't until I turned eighteen that I managed to move the exchange rate to $10 an hour by joining a carwash. I worked during the coldest months of winter, outside, in the frost, my breath steaming as it left my lips. I dried cars, vacuumed carpets, cleaned windows and dashboards, added sprays, creams, and scents, with stiff limbs and pink fingers, one car after another for 20 hours each weekend. I was already in college studying full-time, working hard, but I wasn't enthused about the future. I discovered that graduates earn an average of $33,000 in their first job out of college.[62] It would take years for that number to grow, through long hours and countless promotions, and decades to become meaningful. I saw the goal pyramid in front of me, taller than a skyscraper, besieged with long hours, travel, on-the-job training, and incremental promotions. And looking at the top, an eternity into the future, I didn't like what I saw. *The goal wasn't worth the climb.*

I wanted a better exchange rate between "life" and "cash," but I didn't know how to get it. The only path I saw was the one of college, career, and a multi-decade climb to better wages. I didn't know what any other path looked like. And that's when I began to see a train in the distance – a bright light growing large, rushing forward, full steam ahead. It was the train of disillusionment, coming at me, for me, an inevitable collision between my hopes and dreams and the unrelenting coldness of reality.

Each day the train got closer, pushing through air, towards me, freighted with disappointment, hard and unyielding, an assassin of dreams. I thought back to the man in high school, his brutal speech about going to college, getting an education, becoming somebody. Well, I was in college now, studying full-time, paying my own way, and for what? Where was it taking me?

---

62 Belk College of Business, University of North Carolina at Charlotte, 1998

Certainly not parties in London and Madrid, or champagne in the Eiffel Tower. It was taking me towards $33,000 a year – *$33,000, $33,000, $33,000* – the number became acid in my brain, sloshing around in search for a better exchange rate between life and cash.

I read self-help books; I knew all about saving $287 a month for 40 years to become a millionaire. I was aware of the wide, flat road, the safe one, the one everybody took, the one most people dropped dead on before reaching the end. That road wasn't for me. My impatience flared, my desire made lava look cold. But in the end, that's all it was: *desire.* Animalistic and unthinking, violently hurling itself against rocks and cliffs, no different to the reptiles and sea lions on the Galapagos Islands. I wanted more, but I didn't know how to get more.

As the months passed, the train got very close, blowing its horn, the driver hanging out the window, waving, yelling. I tried to move, I was desperate to move, but my feet were stuck. I wiggled and wrestled, but to no avail. I began sinking to the ground, closer to the dirt, crouching, waiting, the howling train almost upon me. And at the moment of absolute brightness, an imminent train wreck inches away, a miracle happened – the miracle that pulled me from the tracks, saved me from disillusionment, and put success in my hand.

It happened at the gym while the owner was there. He came over for a word, and feeling down, dejected,

I shared my worries with him: the climb from flipping burgers to grocery stores to washing cars, the $33,000 a year I could sell my life for after graduation, the endless stairs I'd have to climb, and the train of disillusionment heading my way. I was lost, I didn't know what to do, where to go. Unhappiness seized me.

"I really don't know much about anything," I told him. "But I know one thing: *I want to be successful, financially successful.* I don't want to be a slave to the dollar."

The owner looked at me, thoughtful, my words not what he was expecting. I was sure he would parrot what everybody parroted: *that's life, that's the way of the world, get used to it.* But he leaned in, close, and said something completely different, something that would change everything.

"I don't know what they're teaching in college these days, but let me tell you one thing. You will *never* become wealthy unless you *own* something. I don't care what – a business, real estate, scientific invention, even a song or painting – but you need to *own* it. The only way you will *ever* become wealthy is by being an *owner*, not a *worker*."

The train threw on its brakes, screeching, sparks flying, steam exploding from the wheels. My feet suddenly grew light. *Something was happening.*

"See that monkey over there," the owner continued, pointing to the boy at the front desk.

"You mean Mark?"

"Yes, Mark."

"What about him?"

"He's a *monkey*. Do you know why?"

I shook my head.

"Because he makes minimum wage. Because he comes in early, leaves at noon, and another monkey takes his place. If he quits, I'll find a new monkey. I'm the *owner*, he's the *worker*. I keep the profits, he does the work. I drive a Porsche and sail in the Caymans, he drives a Chevy and hangs out at the mall. And if he sits at that front desk long enough, staring out the window, he'll begin to wonder why he's not driving a Porsche and sailing around the Caymans. But the answer will always be the same: *because he's a worker, not an owner.*"

He paused for a moment, waving to somebody entering the gym; then his eyes came back to meet mine. "So, you want to become financially successful? Then you need to invest in real estate, the stock market, become an entrepreneur, write a book, or *something*, to become an owner – because you'll *never* get wealthy by being a worker. *Never*." He evaluated the expression on my face, and added, "That's capitalism, my boy. That's the way the world *really* works."

As the owner turned and walked away, brightness began to flood the gym – brightness like I had never known. It came in through windows, doors, in between cracks and holes, reflecting from mirrors, bouncing off walls, dazzling, blinding. It was a supernova, a million floodlights blazing all at once. The man with the whip had been right after all. Knowledge was the answer – *the answer to everything* – becoming successful, wealthy, getting what you want in life.

I picked myself up from the dirt, straightened, and beheld the stars. I could see a new path ahead of me, a new goal pyramid. My lips spread into a smile as I wondered, *What could I own?*

Action Items

I know it's tough. A mortgage, full-time job, kids – some days you're tired and exhausted before you even get out of bed – and you still need to make time for your friends, family, and if there's anything left, yourself. And on top of the time struggle, money struggle, never having enough minutes or dollars, I'm asking you to invest in yourself. It's not easy – *if it was easy, everybody would do it.*

The path to big goals can be tough and unforgiving. And whether you follow it or not depends on desire, *on how much you want it.* If your desire is raging, you'll find the time and money, you'll make whatever investments are necessary, and you'll make them without hesitation. But if you don't – if you pull your wallet off the table and back into your pocket – then your desire is weak. Without desire, you won't make it. It'll be too easy to quit, to stop swimming upstream, to lean backwards and let the current pull you back to where you started.

To walk through the fourth door of success:

- *Discover the path.* Take your three-year goal – the one you defined in the Door of Clarity and later aligned to your desire – and discover the paths that lead to this goal. *How did others achieve what you want to achieve?* You need to find out. All the knowledge you need is available, waiting. And when you compare the different paths, evaluate their risk and other characteristics in the context of your personal situation. Committing everything to your goal may be what you desire most, but the risk might be intolerable, given your family situation and other obligations. Choose a path that best fits your particular circumstances.

- *Create a goal pyramid and invest in yourself.* Once you've chosen a path, break the goal down into milestones using the goal pyramid. Then evaluate each milestone against your current inventory of skills and knowledge. Areas where you are short are areas that require investment. You must do whatever is necessary to achieve the milestones in your goal pyramid. This might mean classroom time, online tutorials, or hands-on-training and instruction, coaching, mentoring – whatever it is, do it.
- *Create weekly tasks.* Each week, create a list of tasks related to the milestones that you're working on. The tasks can be minor – like reading a chapter in a book, attending a workshop, or meeting with someone. The tasks are not goals; they are activities you must complete each week to progress towards the milestones.

The paths to success are varied and many. Nothing illustrates this better than the success and achievement conferences that are put on around the world each year. They showcase a broad spectrum of speakers who have achieved financial success through very different paths, ranging from currency trading and real estate options to life coaching, motivational speaking, franchising, and selling items on eBay. The Door of Knowledge blazes in all its glory as each speaker explains the path they took to reach their particular goals, and the milestones they achieved along the way.

No matter what path you ultimately choose, the process of discovering the milestones and investing in yourself remains the same. You must hunt for success with a club – a club called *knowledge* – because chances are that every problem and obstacle standing between you and your goals has already been solved by someone else.

> *"Vision is not enough, it must be combined with venture. It is not enough to stare up the steps, we must step up the steps."*
> Vaclau Havel

The Fifth Door

What could I own?

The question wouldn't give me rest until an answer was found. At night I could see my past swirling around in circles, formless, dreamy, as through a black and white kaleidoscope. One moment I was stocking shelves in forlorn aisles, flipping burgers on sizzling stoves, and the next I was fighting numbness and wind tears at the car wash. Through the same kaleidoscope I saw the future, equally bleak, of suits and ties, handshakes, office towers, incremental promotions, and monkeys chasing bananas. And in the middle of it all, at the very epicenter, was the flaming question that had turned my life upside down: *What could I own?*

Buying a meaningful asset was out of the question, as my savings were scant. So if I wanted to own something that had value, that could produce income, create wealth, I'd have to *build it*. An idea flirted across my mind, shy and reluctant, fluttering its wings softly on the edge of my consciousness. I considered it, and immediately knew it was the answer: *I would build a business.* On the instant, it became my goal, the thing I wanted to do – and not in ten years or some indefinite time in the future, but *now*, today.

The goal was vague at first, a lighthouse shimmering in the distance, fog-like. But it monopolized my thoughts, pulsing and flashing through purple mists like a puzzle beckoning to be solved. At the university, in class, at the gym between sets and reps, even at the carwash under the crackling heat lamps, I could think of nothing else. My mind was working, churning away, trying to solve the problem I had posed:

What kind of business could I build?

I considered my skills and knowledge. *What did I know? What did I enjoy?* Fitness, nutrition. *What could I do with that?* Become a personal trainer, help others lose weight. *But how could I build a business from personal training?* Start with myself, then hire other trainers. *Yes, that was it!* I would start a personal training business, grow it, then manage the business and keep the profits – *just like the gym owner.* My goal was coming into focus.

I was already in the right environment, in the gym, among bodybuilders and other personal trainers. At the university I joined an entrepreneurs' club of students who were running their own business or wanting to start one. I wrote down my goal of starting a personal training business and mapped out the milestones. There was much to do: incorporate a company, open a bank account, develop a website, print business cards, buy insurance, draft customer contracts, and more.

The largest milestone was *accreditation*, which would enable me to be a "certified" personal trainer. It was a crucial step to earning more money and building a business, but would take nine months to complete – and that was only if I stopped working at the car wash. Nine months without work would decimate my savings, leaving nothing for the program or start-up expenses. Goosebumps ran up my spine as I considered the credit cards in my wallet. *What if I couldn't earn a living through personal training? What if I spent the time and money and found customers hard to come by? What if I failed? What if the business failed? How would I pay off my debts?*

The questions were endless and relentless. But each night, the colorless kaleidoscope played, over and over, like some prison-break movie in which the protagonist fails to escape. *I had to move; now was the time for me to act.* My desire became fire in my veins, forcing me to quit the car wash and spend half of my bank balance on the accreditation program. There was no turning back – I was committed, now. I remembered the man with the whip, his words rattling in my brain like silver coins in a tin can: *invest in yourself, in your education, in your future.* Well, I was investing in myself, no doubt about that, and I was afraid! *Investing was scary* – something the man had forgotten to mention.

As the weeks rolled forward, I studied to become a personal trainer, an entrepreneur, and a college graduate, all at once. Work! Nothing could stop me except my bank balance, which kicked the bucket and forced my credit cards into action. My business expenses were piling up: shirts, insurance, a business telephone, customer contracts, legal liability waivers, and countless other budgetary black holes. My fears mounted as I realized my mistake of underestimating the cost of starting a business. Out of desperation, I applied for student aid, but instead of a government grant, I received a loan – more debt!

I grew restless, stressed. I tossed and turned at night, worrying. I wanted to stop the financial pain. *Should I quit? But what then? What would I do? Go back to the car wash? Finish college and work for $33,000 a year?* No, I couldn't consider that. The spur of desire, painful to the point of drawing blood, wouldn't let me quit. And so I pressed on against the fear, head down, working through the tasks each week, crossing off the milestones, telling everyone about my new personal training business. At night, I would visualize success, seeing my calendar chock full of clients, a healthy bank account, employees working for me, *being an owner.*

I was sprinting through the accreditation courses, but before I could reach the end, my bank account hit empty. I had depleted my student loan and fell back to credit cards. I borrowed money from my parents as a last resort, feeling fear slither around my neck as I did so. I could hear the man with the whip in the faraway distance – *invest in yourself, in your education, in your future* – but his words were faint. I was fighting for air, afraid. No one in my family had ever started a business before; no one could sympathize or assist. I was on my own. Spending time with other entrepreneurs helped, and learning about business – about cash flow, sales and marketing, hiring staff – helped even more. The knowledge empowered me, answered questions, removed doubt.

And then at long last it happened: I became a certified personal trainer, signed my first customer, and began work. Salvation had come. For the first time ever I wore my own shirt on my back, with my own company name and logo, and not somebody else's. "Work" never seemed the same, because I was now working for myself. In time, my bank account reversed course and I began paying down debt, sleeping easy, realizing that all the stress, doubt, and worry *had been worth it.* I looked to the future once more, wanting to build a business that could provide passive income and freedom. The spur of desire was again at my back, prodding me forward, as I set new goals and mapped out the milestones.

In the fifteen years that followed in full color and widescreen splendor, I moved from one goal pyramid to the next, building multi-million dollar businesses, selling them, writing books, speaking at hundreds of events, and winning praise, awards, and wealth in the process. And through it all, I pondered success, wondering why I had achieved it and not someone else. I didn't have any special skills or advantages − I had attended public schools and made average grades, my parents weren't wealthy, no one bankrolled me, I didn't have any close friends who were entrepreneurs, I didn't even have a mentor to provide advice, guidance, or introductions. Anyone could have done what I did, and yet, they didn't.

Why?

What You Do

The self-improvement industry is worth $12 billion annually with more than 45,000 self-help titles in print.[63] Each year, more books are published and more dollars spent. And each year, the poor keep getting poorer. *How poor?* The median American in the bottom quintile of wealth is 63% *poorer* than his counterpart a generation ago, with similar drops in wealth for the next two socioeconomic

---

63 Vanderkam, L., "The Paperback Quest for Joy: America's Unique Love Affair with Self-help Books," *City Journal*, Manhattan Institute for Policy Research, 2012

strata.[64] These are the people buying books, listening to tapes, attending seminars, spending $12 billion on self-improvement each year. *And it's getting them nowhere.*

Why?

Because people aren't looking for the "secrets" to success, they're looking for the "shortcuts" to success. They want to get rich with no risk and no money down; they want to lose weight without diet or exercise; they want to look 20 years younger overnight, through creams, lotion, and glitter. *Effortless, simple, risk-free!* Those are the headlines that sell. *No work required!* And people buy and consume the hype, gorging themselves to the tune of $12 billion each year. They read the books, watch the DVDs, and listen to the seminars. It makes them feel drunk, high. Their feet leave the ground and they space-walk to the moon. Their dreams are alive and well, within reach, *and it's effortless, simple, risk-free* – the books and seminars said so.

But weeks pass, then months, and of course, nothing changes in their life. Each evening they wish upon a Ferrari, and each morning they wake up disappointed. The high eventually wears off and their spacewalk ends, abruptly, like some grotesque hallucination. They fall out of orbit, back down to earth, back to their unchanged reality. And each year the cycle repeats itself: the poor

---

64 Rampell, C., "Richer Rich, and Poorer Poor," *New York Times*, 10 July 2012

and fat consume another $12 billion of self-improvement and end up poorer and fatter than ever before.

The truth is that success requires work, effort, *action*. But people don't want truth – *they want the results without the work*. They want shortcuts, wishful thinking, unwilling to admit that success won't happen by itself. *But think logically for a moment*. Reading fitness books won't make you fit; you must read the books *and take action* – change your diet, start exercising. And attending wealth seminars won't make you wealthy; you must attend the seminars *and take action* – spend less, invest more, start a business. No matter how precise your goals, no matter how great your desire and self-belief, no matter how much knowledge you've crammed into your head, *nothing will happen without action*. Action is the genesis of success – the start, the beginning. Without action, there's no motion. Everything remains frozen, sterile, dead.

Action = results.

Consider this book for a moment. The goal pyramid for *Life in Half a Second* hangs in front of me; my desire is enormous; I know I can achieve the goal; I know what to write and how to write it. *But the book won't write itself*. Unless I take action – unless I sit down each morning and write *Life in Half a Second*, page by page, the book won't exist. And there are thousands of books, millions, that never left their authors' minds – books that could have improved mankind, brought joy and wonder into our lives, inspiration, philosophy, meaning – which are lost, unborn, dead before inception. What's the difference between the library of written books and the library of unwritten books?

Action – the fifth door of success.

Nothing you do in life will amount to anything unless you take action. The preceding four doors are interesting, thought-provoking, but without action they won't change your situation. *Only action can turn your goals into reality.* And no matter how small and difficult the preceding four doors are to walk through, the Door of Action is the smallest and most difficult of them all. It's tiny, microscopic. Most people can't find it, and those who do usually just stare at it. *And why is that?* Why is it so hard for people to take action?

The most obvious reason is a lack of clarity, desire, belief, and/or knowledge. Without clarity, there's no goal to direct your efforts toward. Without desire, you don't want it badly enough. Without belief, you doubt and question yourself, sitting and waiting when you should be standing and acting. And without knowledge, you don't know what to do, or how to do it.

For your actions to be effective, to move you towards your goals, you must walk through *all* the doors of success. Not one or two, *but all of them.* And if you have clarity, desire, belief, knowledge, and still hesitate at the final door, then there's only one reason left: *fear.*

Action and fear

Fear is a tranquillizer, a sedative; it prevents action and holds us back from living a full life. Fear is the reason that people don't take action, the reason they don't pursue dreams, start a business, change jobs, change countries, get married, get divorced, go back to school, and more. When fear is present, the safest thing to do is stand still, do nothing, live in suspended animation. And there are plenty of things to fear these days: failure, change, rejection, criticism, embarrassment, commitment – there's even a *fear of goal-setting* and *fear of success*. No matter how irrational some of these fears may be, the effects are real, with almost $14 billion spent each year in the United States on the treatment of phobias and other anxiety disorders.[65]

It's not surprising that psychology research has demonstrated a strong connection between fear and goal-setting – the greater our fear, the less likely we are to pursue our goals, *or even set goals in the first place.*[66] Recent research has shown that when fear creeps into the mind of the goal-setter, it urges them to return to known, comfortable behaviors and thought patterns.[67] I know this feeling all too well. In everything I did in life, I felt fear.

---

65 US National Institute of Mental Health
66 Elliot, A. J., Church, M. A., "A Hierarchical Model of Approach and Avoidance Achievement Motivation," *Journal of Personality and Social Psychology*, volume 72, 1997
67 Williams, R., "Wired for Success," *Psychology Today*, 11 April 2011

The night before I gave my first public speech in front of a crowd of hundreds, I lay awake in bed, sweating, seeing red, worrying that I would draw a mental blank on stage. I couldn't shake the vision of myself at the podium, engulfed in silence, not remembering what I had just said or what was supposed to come next. The awkwardness was terrifying, like the hiss of an electric chair. I could see the audience staring at me, seconds passing with the speed of snails, as I stood there dumbfounded, self-conscious, leaning against the podium for support.

And when I started my second business after college in the area of financial planning, I spent most days prospecting for new clients. It didn't take me long to fear the telephone. Instead of seeing the handset, I saw rejection, failure, and embarrassing stretches of silence. And years after that, when I moved to Australia and started my fourth company, I asked several people to emigrate with me as co-founders of the new business. When they agreed, fear immediately pulled up a chair and began asking questions: *What if Australia is nothing like the United States? What if your friends move, leaving their jobs and lives behind, and it doesn't work out? What if the business fails?* And when I wrote *Winning Credibility*, fear sat next to me, looking over my shoulder, poisoning my mind: *What if you're no good as a writer? What if the book doesn't get published? What if it doesn't sell? What if readers think it's silly, childish?* Day after day, I sat down at my desk to write, and day after day, fear sat down beside me. Whether it was public speaking, launching a new business, or writing a book, fear never left my side.

The more I've thought about fear over the years, turning it over in my mind, analyzing it, the more I realized that *fear = progress*. Whenever I felt fear, it meant I was making progress, *I was moving towards my goals.* And because my goals were always something new, something I had never done or achieved before, I was always leaving my comfort zone behind and finding myself in a perpetual state of discomfort. Had I stayed stationary in life, in the same business, same country, *same everything*, then my fear would have departed. But it's impossible to achieve success without moving out of our comfort zone, and for that reason, *it's impossible to achieve success without fear.*

From Caveman to Modern Man

During the past two million years, fear has been one of the most important survival mechanisms of the human race.[68] Without fear, we'd be extinct. And because cavemen who possessed a heightened sense of fear were more likely to survive and reproduce, it means we are the offspring of the most paranoid and fearful cavemen that ever lived. The brave and fearless humans who

---

68 Sadava, D., Hillis, D., Heller, C., Berenbaum, M., Life: *The Science of Biology*. W.H. Freeman

explored deep caves, ate unknown plants, slept in the open, and approached wild animals, are no longer part of the gene pool. What's left are the fear-soaked genes that make up the Homo sapiens species as it exists today.

In our climb from flint and fire to the modern age, fear has protected us – it has been a prerequisite for survival. But as our environment changed – as we migrated from caves to cities, no longer fleeing from predators or fighting frost and famine – our heightened sense of fear remained the same. We tend to forget that everything we are today, we inherited. We're still wired for survival, but living in a world where that wiring is working against us. And since there are no wild animals to fear, we direct our survival mechanism in other directions – *the wrong directions* – to fear embarrassment, rejection, failure, criticism, and more.

I sometimes think that the difference between animals and humans is not self-awareness, intelligence, or the presence or absence of a soul, *but in what we fear.* When an animal falls, its fear is centered on its well-being, survival. If they're injured, they may be unable to hunt, escape a predator, or protect their offspring – it might be the end for them. But if a human slips on a banana peel and goes flying into the air, feet up, arms flailing, onto their back in the middle of a busy street, their immediate fear has nothing to do with wellbeing or survival, *but with their self-image.*

Did anybody see me fall? they think. *How embarrassing!*

Humans used to be on par with animals, fearing physical harm above all else. But as we grew civilized and modern, something changed. *That something was marketing.* On a daily basis, through magazines, television shows, billboards, we're told what to eat, drive, wear. The average city dweller sees up to 5,000 advertisements *per day*, convincing them to pay thousands of dollars for handbags, watches, cars, because nothing is more important than self-image.[69] That's why public speaking is the number one fear in the United States – not death, disability, financial destitution, *but public speaking.*[70] The fear of damaging our self-image stands above all other fears – 5,000 advertisements say so each day. We're not worried about wellbeing any more. What's on the inside is far less important than what's on the outside. The clothes and shoes can be uncomfortable, *but as long as they look good, it doesn't matter!*

Through the miracle of modern marketing, we've become exceedingly conscious of our self-image and incredibly fearful of damaging it. And it's precisely this fear that prevents us from speaking in front of packed crowds or asking someone out on a date. We're afraid

---

69 Story, L., "Anywhere the Eye Can See, It's Likely to See an Ad," *New York Times*, 15 January 2007

70 Croston, G., "The Thing We Fear More than Death: Why Predators Are Responsible for Our Fear of Public Speaking," *Psychology Today*, 28 November 2012

of rejection, failure, embarrassment. And the situation is made worse by seeing successful people on television, in magazines – business people epitomizing strength, politicians exuding confidence, actors and models unmarred by a single glimmer of fear. We begin to doubt ourselves, thinking success is impossible because we're not as fearless as them. *But it's a misconception that successful people are fearless.* The capacity to fear is shared by every man, woman, and child that carries the genes of our ancestors – it's the way we've been wired since our caveman days. Those who succeed with eyes wide open, unflinching, are those who have learned to overcome their fears. *You must learn to do the same.* Fear is inevitable on the path to success – you must control your fear or else your fear will control you.

And so the last key to the last door of success is to *conquer your fear*.

You won't achieve anything in life if you remain stuck in your comfort zone, fearful and unwilling to step out. And it's exactly this area that people seem to have the most trouble with. When I speak at conferences about success, preaching that fear must be squashed like so much rotten fruit, I know that the audience is sitting there, thinking, *yes, that all makes sense, but how exactly can I conquer my fear?* Everything I've said thus far – about having precise goals, aligning them to your desire, changing your environment to increase self-belief, and investing in yourself – makes perfect sense.

It's straightforward and easy to grasp. But *conquering fear* — well, that's not so straightforward anymore.

Fear and associations

The first thing to understand about fear is that it can be *learned* and *unlearned*.[71] Psychology research suggests that humans are born with just two basic fears: fear of falling and fear of loud noises.[72] All other fears are learned through experience, education, or observation. If you suffer an accident while cycling on the open road, you may fear riding your bike. But you weren't born with that fear — you *learned* to fear cycling after your accident, in the same way that someone learns to fear dogs after being bitten. The fear of cycling or dogs can also be learned by witnessing a cycling accident or a person being mauled, or by having your parents teach you that cycling and dogs are dangerous. In any case, *the fear is learned*.

You learn to fear rejection, embarrassment, failure, criticism and more, in exactly the same way — mostly through observation. You watch a comedy about some

---

71 This is studied in psychology as fear conditioning, which began with John Watson's famous Little Albert experiment in 1920. It is a form of learning in which an unpleasant stimulus (e.g. electric shock) is associated with a neutral subject (e.g. rabbits), resulting in a fear response to the originally neutral subject (i.e. a person begins to fear rabbits because they associate them with pain)

72 Menzies, R., Clarke, J., "The Etiology of Acrophobia and its Relationship to Severity and Individual Response Patterns," *Behavior Research and Therapy*, 1995; Gibson, E., Walk, R., "The 'visual cliff'", *Scientific American*, 1960

hapless man who makes a fool of himself in front of a crowd, or at the bar while introducing himself to a girl, and you learn to fear those situations. That's where your fears come from, weighing you down throughout life like an anchor that prevents movement and action.

But in the same way that fears are learned, they can also be *unlearned*. They're not permanent characteristics of your personality or psyche – they're malleable, changeable, conquerable. You learn to fear by creating an association between the thing you fear and some negative outcome. After suffering a cycling accident or seeing a friend mauled by a dog, you may associate cycling and dogs with pain. If you fear talking in front of large crowds, you might associate public speaking with embarrassment. If you fear asking someone out on a date, you might associate that activity with rejection. And so on. You can *unlearn* these fears if you change the association.

When I owned a financial planning business, I feared cold calling because I associated it with rejection. Most of my calls were failures. But the only way to build my business was through prospecting for new clients. And what I realized was that even though the majority of my calls ended in rejection, those that didn't had an excellent chance of converting into clients. So every call I made, regardless of the outcome, brought me closer to my next client. *Every call I made brought me closer to a bigger business.* And once my association changed, my fear of the telephone went away. I no longer cared about rejection or embarrassment. What I cared about was building my business, and I was doing that with every call.

Think of the millions of people who would live healthier lives through diet and exercise if they associated those activities with a longer life, more energy, looking younger, being more upbeat – rather than the emptiness of a growling stomach and the burn of lactic acid. The associations we create for ourselves affect the fears we have and the actions we take. When I look at a treadmill, I see health, energy, and long life – *what do you see?*

Biology of fear

The second thing to understand about fear is that it causes a physical reaction in your body through the release of adrenaline and cortisol. This is classically referred to as the "fight or flight" response, characterized by increases in heart rate, blood pressure, muscle tone, and pupil size. You can learn to control this biological response, in the same manner that actors learn to overcome stage fright. The first time I stood on stage and delivered a presentation in front of a large audience, I immediately appreciated the biology of fear. I wasn't in any physical danger behind a podium, and yet, fear manifested itself in the most annoying of ways. My heart pounded wildly as my survival mechanism reacted to dangers and threats that existed only in my mind. Breathing was difficult, putting a quiver in my voice at times that sounded awful. My hands trembled. The heat under my suit intensified until it became an oven.

In my quest to become a better speaker, I studied ways of calming the body and mind: everything from breathing exercises and placing cold objects on my wrist, through to avoiding caffeine and keeping my hands loose. The techniques taught me to become a better speaker, but more importantly, through practice and repetition, they taught me to control the biology of fear. The techniques are available for anyone to learn, including you – if you *want* to.

Revisiting the Past

By learning to change your associations and control your response to fear, you'll be on your way. You'll become conscious of what fear is, where it comes from, and how it affects you. The rest of what you need lies in the preceding four doors of success. Each door has something unique to contribute in your fight against fear.

Fear and clarity

The fundamentals of the Door of Clarity – *setting goals, telling others about them, and visualizing the outcomes* – are potent tools in helping you overcome fear and take action. Research has demonstrated that goals focus your attention and efforts in a particular direction, which means you're more likely to *take action* if you have goals – *especially if you share those goals with others.*[73] If you want to change careers or start a business, fear will be quick to ask you: *What if you don't earn as much? What if you fail? What will your friends think?* But by writing down your goals and sharing them, you're more likely to take action because *you've increased your commitment to take action.*

Besides goal-setting, the Door of Clarity provides visualization as another weapon against fear. If you watch a scary movie over and over, ten or twenty times, what happens? The movie isn't scary anymore because you know what happens next – you've *seen* it before. Visualization works in the same way. By visualizing something a number of times in your mind, your fear is reduced when it comes to the real thing. You're more at ease because you know what comes next – you've seen it before in your mind. It's a proven method for reducing fear and increasing performance, and is widely used in business, professional sports, medicine, and psychology.

When I was striving to improve my speaking skills, every book I read, every speaker I met, said the same thing: visualize the whole event from beginning to end – walking to the stage, up the stairs, to the podium, greeting the audience – *all of it.* When it comes to the actual

---

73 Cummings, T. & Worley, C. *Organizational Development & Change*, South Western Educational Publishing, 2004

presentation, it won't seem new or threatening because you've *seen* it before in your mind. Your survival mechanism won't fire and the event will play out like you imagined. *Visualization works.* Even though visualization can't make a Ferrari materialize in your driveway, it will move you a long way down the path when combined with the other doors of success.

Fear and desire

In the Door of Desire, it's interesting to note that psychologists classify *fear* and *desire* as opposite emotions.[74] Desire is positive, pushing and pulling you towards goals, while fear is negative, paralyzing you with panic and anxiety. This puts additional focus on the central role that desire plays in the pursuit of goals and achieving success. Your desire must be strong enough to catapult you into motion, breaking inertia and complacency, and then strong enough keep you in motion once fear sets in.

In the battle between fear and desire, the strength of your desire will determine the outcome. If your desire is weak, then fear will win. *You want to change careers but fear change. You want to start a business but fear failure. You want to get married but fear commitment.* And so you take the safe option and do nothing. If you *really* wanted to change careers, start a business, or get married – you'd do it.

---

74 Waitley, D., *Psychology of Success*, McGraw-Hill, 2010

No excuses. But because your desire is weak, you let the hand of fear hold you back. To conquer fear, your desire must be rioting in your heart, thrashing and bashing to escape, like a frenzied mob in a cage. That kind of desire will strangle fear. *That kind of desire will make fear fear itself.*

When I was six years old, my parents wanted to escape Communist Poland. They wanted to leave, *but they were afraid.* Escaping Communism meant leaving behind their family, friends, work, culture – *everything* – and moving to someplace new, foreign, with a different language. And if they escaped, they could never come back so long as Communism existed in Poland – it was a one-way trip. Not surprisingly, their fear was enormous; but even more enormous was their desire to escape. *So what happened?* They packed their bags and left. Their desire won the battle.

The psychological battle between fear and desire is exemplified on TV shows such as *Amazing Race, Survivor,* and *Fear Factor.* Whether it's heights or spiders, the contestants must do the things they fear – things they would normally *never* do. In everyday life, they would steer clear of heights and spiders, and yet on the TV show, they're somehow able to overcome their fear. *How?* Think about that for a moment: *how do they overcome their fear?* Through desire. *Their desire to win overpowers their fear.*

What these TV shows demonstrate is that you can conquer fear if your desire is strong enough. Whenever you say "I can't," what you're really saying is "I don't want to." Probably the longest list in the universe is the "can't list," stretching from planet Earth to the black hole in the centre of the Milky Way: "I can't lose weight, I can't make more money, I can't start a business," and on it goes, matched only by the equally long and brilliant list of excuses and explanations: everything from "I feel dizzy when I diet, the economy is bad, I'm not cut out to run a business" through to "my knee hurts, I have a pimple on my nose, it's too cold outside." There is no such word as "can't" – remove it from your vocabulary. If you were burning with desire, you *could* and *would* do the things you "can't." Don't believe me? Then consider the following question:

Could you triple your income in the next twelve months?

No? *Impossible*, you say?

What if your children's lives depended on it? What if your children would die if you didn't triple your income in the next twelve months – could you do it then? *Yes!* Of course you could. If your child's life depended on it, you could earn four times as much if you had to. *So what just happened?* You're not any smarter, your brain is still the same size, you haven't developed any new skills or virtues, you're exactly the same, with the same ten fingers and toes, and yet suddenly, you're able to do something you thought was impossible ten seconds ago.

What changed? *Desire.*

The single variable that changed was your desire to triple your income. So why aren't you earning three times as much right now? Because your desire isn't as strong as it would be if someone's life depended on it. So be honest with yourself and replace "can't" with "don't want to" in your vocabulary. "Can't" is for the lazy, the weak, those who like to be victims and make excuses. Get rid of "can't" from your life. If you don't do something – whether it's changing careers, starting a business, getting married, or losing weight – it's not because you "can't" but because you "don't want to." *Because your desire isn't strong enough.*

Fear and belief

In the Door of Belief, changing your environment can change your self-belief. But changing your environment can also alleviate fear, because it's easier to take action around people who are doing what you fear doing. Think about skydiving, bungee jumping, trekking through the Alps – it's all easier when you're surrounded by people doing the same thing. In addition to supporting one another, the task doesn't seem as threatening because everybody is doing it.

If you fear scorpions and visit a country where everyone eats fried scorpions for breakfast, lunch, and dinner, and everywhere you look, everyone you see, is eating scorpions, what will happen? You'll become de-sensitized to the sight of scorpions, and your fear will recede. And because you're a product of your environment, I'm willing to bet that you'd end up eating scorpions if you lived there. So the tool for fighting fear from the Door of Belief is simple: spend time with people who are doing what you fear doing. *If they can do it, so can you.* You'll be less fearful surrounded by people doing and succeeding at what you fear.

Fear and knowledge

And finally, the Door of Knowledge is instrumental in our fight against fear because we tend to be afraid of what we don't know and don't understand. Consider that when primordial man first saw lightning, he was afraid. *Why?* Because he didn't know what it was. The flashing arches were terrifying, beyond his understanding, so much so that he invented gods to explain them. But when we see lightning today, we're not afraid. We *know* what lightning is, and that knowledge has extinguished our fear. And by the same token, there are many things we still don't know and understand – like what happens after death – so we're still afraid of them.

The process of knowledge conquering fear is best observed in children. Their fear of storms, the dark, animals, and many other things, begins to fade as they grow older *and their knowledge increases.* Even with profound fears, like snakes, spiders, or public speaking, there's a relationship between knowledge and fear – you're less afraid of a snake or spider if you *know* it's harmless. And on public speaking, a Newspoll study of 1206 respondents found that the fear of public speaking was correlated to education levels: 28% of people with only a high school degree nominated public speaking as their worst fear versus 15% of people who had university degrees.[75] The relationship is clear and has stood the test of time: *the more you know, the less afraid you are.*

On your goal pyramid, the milestones you fear the most are likely to be the ones you know the least about. When I was running a supply chain software company in Australia, I came up against a competing product from SAP called *Advanced Planner and Optimiser* (APO). To achieve my goal of dominating the local market, I had to win against SAP and their new product. But the problem was, I didn't know much about APO. So when the question came up in sales presentations – "How is your product different from APO?" – it was followed by silence, because I didn't know. I began fearing sales presentations, knowing that the APO question would come up and I wouldn't have an answer. *So what did I do?* I turned to the Door of Knowledge. I bought books on APO, attended events where APO was discussed, spoke to APO customers – *what was their experience of the product? implementation? results?* and guess what? It wasn't long before

75 *A Quarter of People Fear Public Speaking More Than Dying*, Smart Company, 2008

I became an expert on APO. My fear of making sales presentations went the other way: *I couldn't wait for someone to raise the APO question.* And if they didn't, I raised the comparison myself, showcasing my product's capabilities in a way that couldn't be matched by APO. Knowledge gave me power – the power to conquer my fear.

Besides increasing your store of knowledge, the fourth door of success can help you overcome fear in other ways. One of my favorites is by developing a "backup plan." Taking one class per semester at the university was my first serious backup plan in life. The idea came from my parents, their words still ringing in my ears from decades past: *"…* wouldn't it be smart to have *a backup plan?* You know, *just in case."*

Backup plans provide many benefits, but perhaps the greatest is their ability to conquer fear. By having a backup plan, you know the world won't end if you don't succeed – just like I knew the world wouldn't end if I didn't become a professional bodybuilder. If I failed, I would increase my class load at the university and finish my degree. Such backup plans make action easier because you *know* what will happen if you fail – *your backup plan will happen.*

And lastly, when you discover the different paths to success in the Door of Knowledge, some of these paths will be short but risky, while others will be safe but long. This means the path you choose determines the risk you take – and "risk" often manifests itself as fear. So if you choose a path with tremendous risk, you must cope with the fear that comes with it. *Think about this for a moment.* Think about the fear you'd experience saving $287 a month for 40 years versus betting your house on the roulette wheel. You wouldn't notice fear on the first path, whereas fear might give you a heart attack on the second path.

If your fear is so enormous and paralyzing that nothing seems to help, then you must question the path you've chosen. Consider the worst-case scenario, and if you can't stomach that, chances are you've chosen the wrong path – *the risk is just too high*. Evaluate all the paths to your goals for risk, time, and other trade-offs, and choose the path you're most comfortable with. You'll sleep better knowing you can handle the worst-case scenario.

Fear and regret

The last thing to say about conquering fear is the obvious: *nobody wants to fail* – not me, not you, *nobody*. And because nobody wants to fail, we can easily conclude that if we never try, we can never fail. Life then becomes risk-free. But let me tell you from my heart of hearts, that trying and failing is not failing – *not trying is failing.* The greatest failure you can experience in life is not trying. It's like living without loving. Psychology studies prove this point, demonstrating that in the short term, we regret things we *did*: making a mistake, errors in judgment, taking a risk and failing. But in the long run, over many decades, we deeply regret the things we *didn't do*.[76]

I encourage you to reflect on this when making difficult decisions – decisions that involve fear. Your regrets of inaction will last longer and cut deeper than other regrets because psychologically they're more "open" and boundless: *you'll never know what might have been*.[77] So look at *today* from the perspective of *tomorrow* and ask yourself, *What will I regret more: trying and failing, or not trying at all?* If you try and fail, your regret will be short-lived. But if you never try, your regret will be life-long.

Finis

After achieving my goals for the personal training business while still in college, my mind turned to financial planning and money management. I wanted to apply my finance degree and entrepreneurial experience together, in a new business, and felt the idea take root in my mind and begin its upward climb towards the light. Around this time I also found my soul mate and was soon

76 Greenberg, M., "The Psychology of Regret," *Psychology Today*, 16 May 2012

77 Gilovich, T., Medvee, V.H., "The Experience of Regret: What, When, Why," *Psychological Review*, 1995

married, making plans and setting goals for the future that lay ahead.

But then I met someone who threw a wrench into my well-ordered world, sending bolts and screws flying, and jamming that splendid machine inside my head. Well, I never really *met* Jack London – I only read his books – but through them we shook hands. And as we did so, I realized that Jack London was immortal, that some hundred years after his body gave out his soul lived on, in the dancing light and color of his prose, ever ready to leave its mark on the reader's mind. Jack London had extended his half second into something more – *something eternal*. I looked at his life, then at my plans, and my plans were scorched by the comparison. A profound desire swelled within my heart: *I wanted to write!*

Without warning or invitation, the dream to become an author pushed its way into my dreambox, elbowing aside other goals and demanding a rethink of my future. But my new dream was in competition with my existing goal to become financially independent. My desire for wealth was never a shallow or materialistic quest for riches, nor was it a "game" or way of "keeping score," as I have heard other entrepreneurs describe it over the years. My pursuit of wealth was about one thing, and one thing only: *the equation between "life" and "cash."* I could destroy this equation – permanently bring it to zero – by becoming financially independent. If I had enough wealth, then I would never sell "life" for "cash" again. My life would be my own, and I could spend as much of it as I wanted with my family and doing the "want to" things in life. And because I was aware of this – because Target stores had taught me the value of life – I knew that my desire for financial independence was greater than my desire to write. I wasn't willing to trade my "life" for any other goal.

At heart, I wanted to achieve both goals. But I had a choice: I could try to reach financial success *through* writing, or I could try to reach it through business and *then* write. Put another way, I had a choice between two very different paths in life: ditch business and start writing, climbing up the literary ranks until I sold enough books to become financially independent; or continue as an entrepreneur – starting, growing, and selling businesses to become financially independent – and *then* write. I had to choose between these two paths.

At that point in my life, I had more belief in myself as an entrepreneur than a writer. My personal training business was a success, providing more income and freedom than the $33,000 shackles other graduates had settled for. Knowing business as I now did, I believed it would be easier to become wealthy from business than literature. To learn writing I'd have to start my studies over, and the path to financial independence would be longer and less likely. I was also very young, without much life experience, so even if I dropped everything and began writing, I wouldn't have much to write about. I hadn't seen or done anything yet – my whole life was still in front of me, unlived. I realized that by staying on the entrepreneur's path, I could achieve my financial goals *and* see enough of life to write.

And so I chose the second path, the entrepreneur's path, and in the fifteen years after college, I built and sold four companies. I achieved my financial goals in full, and in the process, observed enough of man, nature, and the cosmic forces of life to write this book and many others. And as I sit by the ocean today, writing, thinking, waves crashing, assembling thoughts and reflections into words and sentences, looking back upon life through a kaleidoscope of flamboyant color, the realization is not lost upon me that I've achieved my first goal and moved on to the second.

It happened so quickly that I often wonder, *How did I get here? What did I do?* But you already know the answer: *I did what's in this book* – nothing more, nothing less. I set goals from my dreambox, changed my environment to match my goals, mapped the path to success, invested in myself, burned the midnight oil acquiring knowledge, and always, *always* took action. Even when I feared it the most. My life turned out the way it did because I designed it that way – it wasn't accidental and didn't happen by chance. I don't say that to impress you or to sound important. I say it because it's true, because I'm proud of it, and *because you can do the same.*

What I've done, you can do. *I've shown you how.* Everything you need to achieve your goals – whatever they may be – is here. There are no other secrets, magic formulas, or shortcuts. *This is it.* Every success book you read, every motivational speaker you hear, will present a variation of what's in *Life in Half a Second.* Whether it's goal-setting and visualization, desire, self-belief, or developing your mind – it all comes back to these five fundamental doors of success. I didn't invent them. I merely observed, analyzed, and distilled them into their simplest form. Then I arranged them into a sequence that you could follow. *That's it.*

Now you know what I know.

And the question is: *What are you going to do with it?*

Action Items

The only person responsible for your success is *you*. Not the government, not the economy, not your parents, but *you*. And if you don't take action to turn your goals into reality, the person it will affect the most is also *you*. So stop procrastinating, looking for excuses, feeling that the world isn't helping you enough. Take ownership of your goals and actions – the only time you'll ever have is now. *Your half second is ticking*.

To walk through the fifth and final door of success:

- *Act!* The easiest way to take action is through your weekly tasks. If you find yourself procrastinating, then break your weekly tasks down into daily tasks. Don't think about the tasks, don't analyze them – *just do them*. The "thinking" takes place earlier, when you're selecting the path and mapping out the milestones. In the Door of Knowledge, you can think, plan, analyze. But once you're down to weekly tasks, you're at the Door of Action and must *do*. The weekly tasks are your only connection to real action – it's where the rubber meets the road. So your objective each week is to cross off the tasks as "done."

- *Consider your milestones.* On your goal pyramid, do any of the milestones give you heartburn? Analyze them from the perspective of the preceding four doors of success – is anything missing? The milestones you associate with fear are often those short on desire, belief, and/or knowledge. Zoom in on these milestones and address any shortcomings, so that they don't block your progress on the goal pyramid.

- *Consider your path and backup plan.* If your fear is greater than any individual milestone, keeping you awake at night, paralyzing your thoughts and actions, then re-evaluate your entire path. Can you stomach the risk? The worst-case scenario? Do you have a backup plan? Is there another way?

- *Replace "can't" with "don't want to."* Every time you use the word "can't," you're lying to yourself and those around you. "Can't" chips away at your self-belief; "can't" sabotages your desire and actions; "can't" is a deadly venom you must extract from your life. Be honest with yourself and use the words "don't want to" instead. Stop making excuses to mask your lack of desire: either you "want to" or "don't want to" – there is nothing in between. *There is no such thing as "can't."*

Successful people are successful because they know what's in this book – either through learning and living, like me, or instinctively, through some sixth sense. In either case, they succeed because of these five doors of success. And no matter what your personal circumstances are, you can do the same. It's not rocket science, it's right here in black and white, step by step. Countless people have already done it. All you need to do is *take action*.

The choice is yours; the future is yours. *What happens next is up to you.*

"Behold, I have lived!"
Jack London

Waking Up ...

In the silent watches of the night, when you're fast asleep, dreaming, your strangest and most bizarre experiences come to life. You can be in bed one moment, warm, snug, fuzzy, eyes sealed tight, and then in outer space the next, flying to the moon, fighting aliens. Unprompted, random, uncontrolled, emerging from nowhere and disappearing into amnesia, your dreams are without limit, playing like a montage, pairing forgotten bosses and former lovers together, hand in hand, cheek to cheek, dancing and fading against a backlot of frozen plains and avalanches – all without conflict, ingeniously congruent. And upon waking you think, *what a strange dream!* You marvel at the strangeness, scratching your head for some deeper meaning – wondering what your subconscious is trying to say.

But dreams only seem strange *after* you wake up. They don't seem strange while you're dreaming *because you don't know that you're dreaming.* No matter how strange, pigs flying or aliens attacking, your dreamscape is your reality until you wake up and re-enter the real world.

But isn't the "real world" just as strange as your strangest dream?

Consider that we're inside an unfathomably large cosmic structure we don't understand, can't measure, can't comprehend, which is expanding at the rate of more than 40 miles per second per Megaparsec.[78] Recent research into the movement of galaxies suggests that something immeasurably large lies *beyond* the borders of our visible universe, pulling more than one thousand *galaxies* towards it like water down a drain. Dubbed "the dark flow," it's so powerful that nothing we know about the universe can account for it.[79] Just like a dream, *we don't know where we are, where we came from, or where we're going,* but nobody seems to think that's strange.

Our unit of measure is "time," which has no beginning and no end, and which is oddly affected by speed and gravity – so much so that atomic clocks on satellites in space move faster than atomic clocks on Earth and

---

78 Ringstrom, A., "Speeding Universe Work Wins Nobel," *Reuters*, 4 October 2011; NASA; and Atkinson, N., "Spitzer Provides Most Precise Measurement Yet of the Universe's Expansion," *Universe Today*, 3 October 2012

79 Scientists Detect Cosmic "Dark Flow" Across Billions of Light Years, Press Release, NASA, 23 September 2008; and Roach, J., "New Proof Unknown 'Structures' Tug at Our Universe," *National Geographic*, 22 March 2010

must be recalibrated.[80] And our ever-accelerating universe and "time" are somehow related, even combined, into a physical fabric called the "space-time continuum," which our planet sits on and "drags" as it spins through space. Scientists have recently measured the so-called "frame-dragging" effect, which is the distortion our planet creates in the space-time continuum as it orbits the Sun – a distortion strong enough to push probes out of orbit by nearly seven feet due to "ripples" in the space-time "carpet."[81] *This isn't science fiction* – this is our world, our reality, the one we live in *now*.

Some physicists are uncovering more dimensions on top of the traditional four we grew up with – theorizing that countless "parallel universes" could exist with identical versions of ourselves[82] – while other physicists are assembling the first quantum computers to harness the power of sub-atomic particles that *can exist in two places at the same time*.[83] All this is on top of "mundane" discoveries, such as a diamond planet found by researchers at Yale University that's estimated to be worth $26.9 *nonillion*

80 Ashbury, N., "Relativity in the Global Positioning System," *Living Reviews in Relativity*, Max Planck Institute for Gravitational Physics, 28 January 2003

81 "Einstein's Warp Effect Measured," BBC News, 21 October 2004

82 Chalmers, M., "Stringscape," *Physics World*, 3 September 2007

83 Connor, S., "Einstein was right, you can be in two places at once," *The Independent*, 17 December 2010

dollars according to Forbes,[84] or a huge cloud near the center of our galaxy made almost entirely of raspberry-flavored rum, containing *10 billion billion billion* liters of alcohol.[85]

And yet, none of these things seem "strange" to anyone. We go on with our lives, working, eating, sleeping, in sheer oblivion, like ants in an aquarium, floating through something, somewhere. *But I think it's strange.* Having run two software companies, the universe reminds me of a computer program that's being written and executed at the same time. But I'm in no position to question anything because my perspective is hopeless.

Why?

Because my eyes can see less than 1% of the electromagnetic spectrum and my ears can hear less than 1% of the acoustic spectrum.[86] And even if I could see and hear the whole spectrum, it wouldn't do me any good, because 96% of everything in the universe cannot be seen or measured by *any* instrument we've invented thus far. That's right – all the stars, planets and galaxies that can be seen today make up just 4% of the universe. The other

---

84 "Nearby Super-Earth Likely a Diamond Planet," *Yale News*, 11 October 2011; and Cohan, P., "Diamond Planet Worth $26.9 Nonillion," *Forbes*, 12 October 2012

85 Sample, I., "Galaxy's Centre Tastes of Raspberries and Smells of Rum, Say Astronomers," *The Guardian*, 21 April 2009; and Whitehouse, D., "Alcohol Haze at Galactic Heart," BBC News, 9 October 2001

86 "We Originated in the Belly of a Star," *Lunar Science Institute*, NASA

96% is made of stuff astronomers can't see, detect, or even comprehend, appropriately named "dark matter" and "dark energy" because we're in the dark about what's really out there.[87]

So with my 1% eyes and 1% ears, living for half a second on a speck of dust, floating through a universe where nearly everything is invisible, my perspective is hopeless. If I lived for a billion years, or was as tall and wide as the Milky Way, then I might have perspective; then I might observe something. But my half second is no different to the lifespan of a mayfly, living and dying inside a single day; never seeing the sun rise or set, never seeing snow, or the seasons change, or owls take flight in the dead of night. Mayflies will never have perspective, and by never having perspective, they will never know *where they are, where they came from, and where they're going.*

The universe is so strange – so inexplicably strange – that perhaps it's all a dream after all? The "real world" is certainly stranger and more bizarre than the strangest and most bizarre opium dream. So who's to say? But if life *is* a dream and you suddenly woke up, *would you be happy with your dream?* Would you wake up knowing you made the most of it? *Or would look back with regret, wishing you had done more?* Wishing you had defined your life and goals more clearly? Made the most of your "days left"?

---

87 Moskowitz, C., "What's 96 Percent of the Universe Made Of? Astronomers Don't Know," Space.com

Followed your deepest desires? Believed yourself capable of doing anything, fearing nothing?

But what difference does it make whether life is a dream or not? Why not do those things anyway? What reason could there be *not to*? Why not use your half second to do something extraordinary? Why not climb mountains, write the ultimate opera, find true love, heal the sick, change the world, help the poor, explore the unknown, and do everything you "want to"? Why not live life like it's a dream? Why not? Why not? *Why not!* You have everything to gain and nothing to lose.

So live, damn it, live!

Be in a hurry to live. Live each day like it's a dream. *Live each year like it's your last.* Enjoy life down to the last drop, the last taste, the very last millisecond. Because dream or not, you only have half a second – so make the most of your days left, do everything you want to, and do it now, before it's too late, *before you wake up ...*

Index

A page number followed by "n" refers to the footnote on that page.

About the Author

Matthew is an international expert in entrepreneurship, innovation, and success psychology. He has established boards that include former heads of state, Nobel Peace Prize winners, and Fortune 500 CEOs, and has a track record of starting businesses from scratch and selling them for tens of millions of dollars.

From 2005–12, Matthew was the co-founder and CEO of SolveIT Software, a supply chain optimization business he grew from zero to almost 180 employees and $20 million in revenue before selling the business to Schneider Electric. Under his leadership, SolveIT Software became the third-fastest-growing company in Australia in 2012, as ranked by Deloitte. The company won numerous awards, and counted among its customers some of the largest corporations in the world, including Rio Tinto, BHP Billiton, and Xstrata.

From 1999–2003, Matthew was the co-founder and CEO of NuTech Solutions in the USA, where he raised more than US$15 million in venture capital and grew the business to almost 200 employees in six international offices. Matthew established an "A-list" board of directors, which included former President of Poland and Nobel Peace Prize winner, Lech Walesa, former National Security Advisor to the President of the United States, Zbigniew Brzezinski, former Bank of America Chairman and CEO, Hugh McColl Jr, and world-renowned fraud expert and subject of Steven Spielberg's blockbuster *Catch Me if You Can*, Frank Abagnale. NuTech Solutions was acquired by Netezza Corporation, which was subsequently acquired by IBM Global Services.

From 1994–99, Matthew was the founder and operator of *Fitness Forever*, a personal training business, and later, the co-founder of *CFG Investments*, a money management and financial planning company with more than $150 million under management.

Matthew's business achievements have been recognised by countless publications, including *Time Magazine, New York Times, Newsweek*, and *Forbes*. He was named the *Pearcey Foundation* "Entrepreneur of the Year," *Business Journal* "40 under 40" list of accomplished business leaders, University of North Carolina "Alumnus of the Year," and Ernst and Young "Entrepreneur of the Year" finalist.

Matthew is the author of several books, including *Life in Half a Second, Winning Credibility, Puzzle-Based Learning*, and *Adaptive Business Intelligence*, and lectures at the University of Adelaide as a Visiting Fellow on the subject of technology commercialization.

For more information, visit www.Michalewicz.com.au

Lightning Source UK Ltd.
Milton Keynes UK
UKHW030715291118
333181UK00010B/150/P